# WHAT WE TALK ABOUT WHEN WE TALK ABOUT CLONE CLUB

# WHAT WE TALK ABOUT WHEN WE TALK ABOUT CLONE CLUB

## BIOETHICS AND PHILOSOPHY IN ORPHAN BLACK

### GREGORY E. PENCE, PhD

AN IMPRINT OF BENBELLA BOOKS, INC.
DALLAS, TEXAS

BenBella Books, Inc.
10300 N. Central Expressway, Suite #530, Dallas, TX 75231
www.benbellabooks.com | Send feedback to feedback@benbellabooks.com

Printed in the United States of America
10 9 8 7 6 5 4 3 2 1

Library of Congress Cataloging-in-Publication Data
Names: Pence, Gregory E.
Title: What we talk about when we talk about clone club : bioethics and
  philosophy in Orphan black / Gregory E. Pence.
Description: Dallas, Texas : Smart Pop, 2016.
Identifiers: LCCN 2015046218 (print) | LCCN 2016002881 (ebook) | ISBN
  9781942952343 (paperback) | ISBN 9781942952350 (electronic)
Subjects: LCSH: Orphan black (Television program) | Bioethics on television.
  | BISAC: PERFORMING ARTS / Theater / History & Criticism. |
  PHILOSOPHY / Ethics & Moral Philosophy. | SOCIAL SCIENCE /
  Popular Culture.
Classification: LCC PN1992.77.O75 P46 2016 (print) | LCC PN1992.77.O75
  (ebook) | DDC 791.45/72—dc23
LC record available at http://lccn.loc.gov/20150462183

Editing by Leah Wilson and Vy Tran | Copyediting by James Fraleigh
Proofreading by Chris Gage and Michael Fedison
Text design and composition by Silver Feather Design
Full cover by Sarah Dombrowsky
Front cover and interior illustrations by Ralph Voltz
Printed by Lake Book Manufacturing

Distributed by Perseus Distribution | www.perseusdistribution.com
To place orders through Perseus Distribution:
Tel: (800) 343-4499 | Fax: (800) 351-5073 | E-mail: orderentry@perseusbooks.com

Significant discounts for bulk sales are available. Please contact Aida Herrera
at aida@benbellabooks.com.

# Contents

## CHAPTER 1

# Orphan Black and Bioethics

B ioethics is one of today's most exciting new fields. *Orphan Black* is one of the most exciting shows on television. Bioethics explores ethical issues in medicine and science. *Orphan Black* dramatizes ethical issues in medicine and science. What could be more appropriate than a marriage of the two? Like the two interwoven strands of nucleotides that make up DNA molecules, the famous "double helix," they are intimately linked.

Bioethics erupted into the consciousness of North Americans in 1962 with a *LIFE* magazine article about the God Committee, which controversially decided on the basis of social worth who lived, and who died, in getting access to then-scarce kidney dialysis machines. As science and technology became more advanced, so did the ethical issues surrounding them: the questionable status as living persons of comatose patients with brain-stem reflexes such as Karen Ann Quinlan, Nancy Cruzan, and Terri Schiavo; legal decisions about abortions; debates about heart transplants, surrogate mothers, AIDS, the vulnerability of psychiatric patients, greedy Big Pharma, Dr. Kevorkian, "Octomom," research on animals, and Obamacare; treatment of intersex, gay, and transgender persons; and enhancements of people by drugs, surgery, and (of special relevance to *Orphan Black*) genetic interventions.

Then, of course, there looms the mega-bioethical issue of our times: cloning humans. From the moment in 1997 that banner headlines screamed about the cloning of Dolly the sheep, the world has been fascinated with the possibly horrific implications of human clones. Perhaps no other ethical issue in modern history has grabbed more attention, caused more hysteria, or inspired so much imaginative film and literature.

*Orphan Black* quintessentially dramatizes human cloning. By placing a clone, Sarah Manning, at the center of the story, and surrounding her with clone sisters and brothers from Projects Leda and Castor as well as the political and religious groups vying to control them, there is just no way the show could avoid engaging with cloning's profound moral questions. Through the Emmy-worthy acting of Tatiana Maslany and a science-driven plot, *Orphan Black* raises issues about living at the edge of what it means to be a human, investigates the impact of nature and nurture on personality and character, and asks profound social and ethical questions about personal identity: How do our birth origins (whether we are created sexually, via assisted reproduction, or cloning) affect who we are? How does being gestated by a surrogate affect us later? What is it like to have not just one identical twin, but *eight* or *fourteen* identical twins? What if you and those twins are raised apart, with different parents and in different cultures? What happens if you are all raised together, like the Castors?

I have spent forty years in bioethics, thirty-four teaching in a medical school. Rare is the time in a professor's life when a television show comes along that highlights the big issue of his or her career. Even rarer is when that same issue is one that has grabbed the world's fascination and horror.

Before *Orphan Black* appeared, I wrote several books about human cloning and gave a hundred talks about it around the world. But cloning humans always seemed so abstract to people; the issue lacked human context. Conversations spring from fears and fantasies, not science and realism. People fear that the emergence of clones would mean inevitable descent into a dystopic, *Blade Runner*–style future. So *Orphan Black*, and the opportunity it provides as a major television drama to discuss human cloning, seemed too good to be true. Suddenly, I had a likeable character—multiple likeable characters!—who had been created by cloning. Not a "clone" or a soulless, *Night of the Living Dead*–style zombie, but a living, breathing, feeling, and yes, sexy, human being. Sarah Manning and her "sestras" (as Ukrainian-raised Helena refers to her clone "sisters") provide that human context, a way to get viewers to see that maybe people could be created through cloning and the sky wouldn't fall.

Actually, using *Orphan Black* to write about ethical issues is a nice compromise between discussing cloning abstractly and trying to imagine real clones in our midst. The difficulties that the sestras face are not exactly real because *Orphan Black* is, in the end, a *fictional* show. On the other hand, its scenes and action don't feel like desert island cases that could never occur. They feel real and urgent.

Nor does this usefulness go only one way. Looking at *Orphan Black* through the lens of bioethics can also enrich our understanding of the show's characters and story line, and what is at stake for and in them.

Regardless of what season four holds for the show (and I hope many seasons beyond that), the existing three seasons contain more than enough material to discuss not only all the ethical issues of human cloning, but many other issues in modern bioethics as well, from genetic engineering to medical experimentation to the commercialization of life itself—all of which we'll talk about in this book.

**CHAPTER 2**

# Personhood and Human Clones

## The Orphans of Project Leda

O *rphan Black* upends the most important, age-old myth about human cloning: that beings originated in this novel way would not be people, but zombies, sex slaves, robots, or property. From the very first scene of this binge-worthy series, when we watch con artist Sarah Manning witness the suicide of her clone-sister, detective Beth Childs, we understand that we are dealing with real humans with the complex fears, ambitions, and loves of humans anywhere on the planet.

Despite the fact that the Dyad Institute, the Neolutionists, and the Proletheans *do* think this way, *do* think of the orphans as "mere clones," *do* think of them as property, as "theirs," we viewers know better. Sarah is just as much a person as the smug, confident Dr. Leekie (unless, of course, we discover one day that, like Rachel Duncan, Leekie was also a clone? Wouldn't that be a kick? A master clone scientist overseeing groups of cloned men and women?). Cosima is just as much a real, human graduate student as any other human grad student. Stepford-like housewife Alison is just as caught up in her children's soccer games as any other suburban mother. Even Rachel, the kapo over the Leda sisters, is familiar to us as the repressed, cold, amoral, controlling, insanely ambitious businesswoman.

In short, although very different in personality and character, the orphans of Project Leda are all *people* originated by cloning, not just mindless clones. Similarly, the cloned men of Project Castor are not a mindless army, but also real, flawed people—if ones raised in unusual circumstances. And as people, the Ledas and Castors possess the same free will to make decisions, the same passion to enter into relationships, the same empathy to mourn the deaths of those they love, and even the same despair to commit suicide.

Why, then, in popular thinking, are clones thought of as something like zombies? Indeed, many people object to human cloning in part because they believe that any being produced this way would be subhuman and treated as such. Why do we assume that beings created without sex would somehow be different—and, more important, different in a *bad* way?

The influential essay about human cloning "The Wisdom of Repugnance," by conservative bioethicist Leon Kass, emphasizes how human clones strike us: "'Offensive.' 'Grotesque.' 'Revolting.' 'Repugnant.' 'Repulsive.'" These are the words most commonly heard regarding the prospect of human cloning. Such reactions come both from the man or woman in the street and from the intellectuals, from believers and atheists, from humanists and scientists. Even Dolly's creator has said he "would find it offensive to clone a human being."

Kass accepts, and even champions, the emotional responses of Luddites and religious conservatives whose guts tell them that human cloning is a *boundary crossing*, a deep violation of human nature, a line that only God and not humans should cross. What is inherently wrong for Kass about the creation of Dolly is what is inherently wrong about the creation of human clones: Dolly "is the work not of nature or nature's God, but of man, an Englishman, Ian Wilmut, and his fellow scientists." Cloned human beings, Kass says, would be the product "of man playing at being God."

Kass and other conservative bioethicists also worry that beings created by cloning would be treated as *commodities*, denied—or unworthy of—the same rights and protections as "normal" beings. As Kass writes, "It is not at all clear to what extent a clone will truly be a moral agent."

The frequency with which critics of cloning refer to it as "manufacture" also attests to the belief that clones would be *less than* human. The word choice invokes a powerful image from Aldous Huxley's 1932 novel, *Brave New World*: babies who emerge on an assembly line, mechanically and uniformly, unwanted, uncherished, un-nurtured, and unloved by normal parents, who hence grow up psychologically malformed.

However, these beliefs are the product of mindless prejudice, a groundless fear based on ignorance of how cloning works (a topic we'll discuss further in later chapters). They also disregard an important principle of modern ethics: that how a human baby is created does not affect its status as a person, either legally or ethically. Put a little differently, it is a widely accepted principle of many ethical theories that people should be treated equally as persons unless there is a relevant reason to treat them differently.

Treating people differently requires special moral reasons. If a professor treats one student in class differently than another, then there must be a morally relevant reason for the differential treatment, such as that the student has a learning disability and so needs extra time taking a test. So just because someone's biological parents were not married or are from different races is not a morally relevant reason to treat children differently who come from such unions. Similarly, just because children were created from assisted reproduction—which one could argue is no more unnatural than cloning—does not mean that, as children or adults, they are anything less than full persons.

If I meet someone who looks, talks, and acts like a person, if I meet Sarah Manning or Krystal Goderitch, then I should—all other things being equal—treat them as persons.

And so we should treat the orphans. Call this the Principle of Non-Discrimination by Origins.

Historically, humans have been slow to learn this fundamental lesson of ethics. Indeed, primitive humans have used skin color, religious beliefs, geographical location, country of origin, marital status of parents, and sexual orientation as reasons to discriminate against others. But modern thinkers, too, have found it difficult to understand, especially when it comes to cloning humans.

According to Nigel Cameron, a famous, modern-day Christian bioethicist, "[Human cloning] would be perhaps the worst thing we have ever thought of in the maltreatment of our species. It would be a kind of new slave class. You would have human beings who were made by other human beings for their purposes." But this is a bad, circular way of arguing. Because other people are prejudiced, it suggests, we must act as if the evil effects of that prejudice are justified. Just because people fear that cloned humans would be evil, unnatural, or weird does not mean that they should be treated differently—unless and until we have real evidence that they are different. And just as we cannot cite prejudice against gay people getting married or interracial marriage as a reason to oppose such marriages, so we cannot cite primitive fears about cloned people as justification for not allowing clones to be born.

A simple corollary of the Principle of Non-Discrimination by Origins holds that no one should suffer prejudice because of how she came into existence. Whether the Project Castor men were conceived in a Petri dish, by an older woman and a younger man, or as twins, triplets, or octuplets should not affect the moral status of each once he enters the world. How and why children arrive in the world does not affect their status as human beings, and they should be treated accordingly.

Legally speaking, as Professor Kerry Lynn Macintosh of the Santa Clara School of Law tells us in her book on human cloning, once a human fetus is viable and living outside the womb, it is a person. Killing a mother carrying a fetus is not a double homicide; killing mother and baby is. This is equally true of children created by various forms of assisted reproduction. No state has ever declared that a child created in a different way is anything less than legally entitled to all the benefits of any child created by sexual reproduction.

With this in mind, let us return to the idea, pervasive in our culture, of clones as commodities or slaves, abused because of their unique origins—and in particular, the idea that the bodies of cloned humans might be salvaged for organs to help their human genetic sources. It's an idea we see repeatedly in literature and film, from the 1976 novel (and 1978 film) *The Boys from Brazil* to the 2005 movie *The Island* and Kazuo Ishiguro's 2005 novel, *Never Let Me Go*.

In case it is not immediately obvious: IT'S WRONG TO MURDER PEOPLE. It's wrong to take away the future life of any living person because you want something from that person, even if that person was created in a different way (a lesson that Tomas and Dr. Virginia "Mother" Coady clearly need to learn).

Why not? Let's take an example. Why can't the child created from Brad Pitt's genes be used later by Brad to replace one of his failing kidneys? After all, without Brad, this child wouldn't exist. Isn't it better, as in the 2005 film *The Island*, to have decades of idyllic life and then be painlessly terminated for organ harvesting than to not exist at all?

Well, the answer is the same as why we can't force an adult to give his or her identical twin with kidney failure one of his healthy kidneys. It would be very nice for the healthy twin to do so—in fact, the first live adult kidney donation, in 1954, was from one such twin to another. But the donation was a *voluntary* decision by the healthy twin, not a forced or assumed one.

Try this another way: Suppose physicians during early pregnancy could give a woman a twinning pill—one that causes her embryo to divide and become two identical embryos, mimicking what sometimes happens without intervention in the case of identical twins—and both embryos are then gestated to birth. Suppose a mother and her doctor conspire that it will be good one day for the first twin to have a "spare parts" twin—and how can the second twin object? Otherwise she would never have existed!

Simply because a person is created by asexual reproduction as spare parts for an ancestor does not mean that, in the words of the great philosopher Immanuel Kant, that person can be used as a "mere means" to sustain the life of his or her genetic source. You cannot and should not create a cloned twin of yourself to become an organ warehouse for your later use.

What happens to Katja Obinger and the Helsinki Ledas of *Orphan Black* is not a "disposal" or a "rendering" of a clone. No, instead, it is, quite plain and simply, *murder.* And if you don't see this, well, you are still not thinking of beings created by asexual reproduction as real people.

In short, clones—whether those created for organ harvesting or scientific purposes like the orphans of *Orphan Black*, or those created by normal, childless couples wanting children with strong genetic connections—would not be mindless zombies, slaves, or commodities (or at least ethically they should not be). They would be people, with all the normal ethical and legal rights of real persons.

CHAPTER 3

# Our Fears of Clones

## And Their Reflections in Literature and Film

With the personhood of clones firmly established, let's take a closer look at some of our cultural fears about cloning humans that underlie the prejudices discussed in the previous chapter, especially those reflected in literature and film.

In looking at whether scientists should be allowed to create cloned human embryos for experimentation, the United States government's Human Research Embryo Panel concluded in 1994 that "popular views of human cloning derive from science fiction books and films that have more to do with cultural fantasies than actual scientific experiments." However, that very fact is why those science fiction books and films are important and worth engaging. In his Senate testimony about a bill to allow such experimentation on cloned human embryos, Boston University law and public health professor George Annas faulted this panel for ignoring the lessons of science fiction, saying they had attempted "to sever science from its cultural context. Literary treatments of cloning help inform us." His larger argument was that these literary treatments should lead us to consider cloning technology too dangerous when applied to humans, but his point about the "cultural context" of cloning remains compelling. By understanding this "cultural context," we can better understand objections to cloning, and the fears that lie behind them.

Here are the four most common cultural fears about human cloning, taken from examples in literature and film:

**First, there is the fear we have touched on already: that the clone would be treated badly, for example, as a slave, conditioned killer-soldier, or source of organ parts.** Such fears center on assumptions that a cloned being would be, or at least be considered, a sub-person, or subhuman. The same fear manifests itself theologically in the fear that clones would lack souls.

Ridley Scott's *Blade Runner*, a classic science fiction film based on Philip K. Dick's novel *Do Androids Dream of Electric Sheep?*, explores this first fear. Though *Blade Runner*'s replicants are not technically clones but androids, they possess many characteristics that human clones would have. They walk, talk, look, act, and feel exactly like humans, while still being considered less than human by the society that created them.

In *Blade Runner*, the Tyrell Corporation's replicants mimic human beings so closely that the two can only be distinguished through elaborate biological tests for emotional responses. Despite this, replicants are slave labor in the hazardous conditions on off-world planets, exploited for exploration there. On meritocratic or egalitarian principles, such beings should possess equal rights as humans; replicants are superior in strength, endurance, and intelligence, but they are treated worse than pets, more like rocks. For replicants to return to Earth is illegal, on pain of death. Without hearing or trial, any replicant caught on Earth can be killed by the Blade Runners, a special police unit. Such executions are not referred to as deaths; rather, replicants are merely "retired," like old pieces of equipment.

We also see this fear of clones being exploited, if less starkly, in the 2005 movie *The Island*. In it, human clones frolic on an artificial island until their rich ancestors need their organs—a fate all the more horrifying, perhaps, for the superficial luxury of the clones' lives. Similarly, in *Never Let Me Go*, the dystopian 2005 tale by Japanese novelist Kazuo Ishiguro, students in a special boarding school learn they are clones being kept to replenish the organs of older, genetically identical ancestors. And Greg Egan's famous 1990 short story, "The Extra," shows a futuristic society where super-rich protagonist Daniel Gray clones mentally challenged copies of his own body. The story opens with Gray showing off to guests five copies of his body, each a decade older than the next. The "Extras" are paraded around a swimming pool like prized pets and kept on leashes and collars. When his original body deteriorates, Gray has doctors transplant his memory and brain into a younger Extra.

In *Orphan Black,* this fear of clonal exploitation manifests in three ways: first, the way that people behind the Leda and Castor Projects regard their "orphans" as their property, secretly monitoring and tagging them and even *patenting* their DNA; second, the way that the Castors are raised to be used as super soldiers; and third, the way that Sarah, Helena, and Kira's unexpected ability to heal is treated by Topside and Dr. Coady's superiors as something like an oil gusher— a major bonanza to be exploited.

A species of this first-fear is the worry that, despite the best efforts of parents and society, cloned children would feel, when they discovered their origins, inferior in comparison to other, "ordinary" children who were created sexually. Such fears of being different, of being marginalized, are reported by some non-heterosexual and transgender people when discovering their sexual or gender identities. So it is not that cloned children would *in fact* be inferior that is the problem, but that others and they themselves might *perceive* being cloned as inferior.

We see this fear in the Leda clones themselves. As Alison tells Sarah bitterly, early on in episode three of season one, "We're clones! We're someone's experiment and they're killing us off!" Felix and Sarah, who each already felt marginalized by society before discovering Sarah's origins, often perceive the Ledas' ultra-marginalized status. And Tony, the transgender Leda, wants nothing to do with the idea that he is a clone, running away from the idea and his sisters.

**A second fear is the opposite of the first one (which reveals how contradictory our feelings are about human clones): that clones would be not subhuman but super-human.** This is also the fear that technology will easily get out of control, that the (cloned) servant will get too strong and turn on the master.

This fear that clones will become too powerful and attack us is front and center in *Cyteen,* C. J. Cherryh's classic 1988 trilogy about human cloning. In it, probes transport humans to distant stars, but it can take a lifetime to get there, so most people stay on Earth. When this new civilization needs more humans, its research foundation, the Reseune Corporation, develops artificial womb tanks to grow cloned humans, called "Azis."

Over three centuries, the off-world peoples and the Azis of the Cyteen star system grow culturally distant from the people of Earth, who are beset by overpopulation, ancient ethnic disputes, and parochial concerns. When Earth declares war, writes Cherryh, "Reseune [cloned] soldiers, then, grim and single-minded and intelligent, oh, yes, bred and refined and honed, knowing by touch and reflex what they had never seen in their lives, knowing above all what their purpose was. Living weapons, thinking and calculating down one track." These soldiers are the literary precursors of the Castors.

(Of course, like the Castors and Ledas, the Azis develop in unexpected ways. Some citizen-humans have Azi-twins and love them as human twins. Predictably, and reflecting our fears that clones would be exploited, most inhabitants of Cyteen treat such Azis as slaves or, in Kant's terms, as a "mere means.")

Interestingly, this fear of clones as superhuman is often accompanied by a concern that said clones would not have a unique identity. We see this with the Castors, who, bred and raised together, seem to have trouble forging separate identities—manifesting most obviously in the scene when Rudy is having sex with a woman and Seth suddenly appears in bed wanting to join in. Rudy and Seth seem to think it perfectly natural that they should share every experience, including sex.

This fear that a cloned child would not have a unique identity also appears in Kate Wilhelm's *Where Late the Sweet Birds Sang*, written at the height of a wave of clone furor and novelized in 1976. The novel explores the tension when one human attempts to forge an individual self separate from her identical half-dozen twins (a problem we'll discuss in more depth later). Genetically identical, gestated together in womb-tanks, and raised under the same conditions, these siblings cannot stand to be apart from one another and feel traumatized when any one of their group is missing.

Wilhelm's novel also presages assumptions in *Orphan Black* about the Castors: that it makes sense to talk of multiple copies of a genotype who are raised together as therefore thinking as a group, that human clones would be poor at thinking for themselves, and that particular types of humans could be created for specific jobs, such as the military.

**Third is the fear that the scientists and physicians behind cloning are not motivated by altruism (e.g., helping infertile people have children) but by greed, arrogance, or an intellectual drive untempered by compassion for those that could be hurt by their work.** This fear paints scientists with a broad brush of moral insensitivity. Drs. Aldous Leekie, Virginia "Mother" Coady, Dyad physician Alan Nealon, and Dyad executive Marion Bowles all perfectly fit this stereotype.

Before he commits sucide in front of his clone daughter Rachel, scientist Ethan Duncan reveals to her that the reason she can't have the children she wants is that he made the Ledas sterile by degrading their endometria with an autoimmune disease. (In this regard, he tells Rachel, "Sarah is not a success but a failure.") "Unfortunately," as Ethan says, "we didn't foresee the consequences" of introducing this autoimmune disease to the Ledas—namely, that the Ledas would also grow polyps on their lungs, kidneys, uteruses, and elsewhere, and that such growths would kill many of them—as they killed Jennifer and were sickening Katja before Helena shot her. This is precisely the kind of failure from epistemological arrogance that literature and movies have always taught us to fear in scientists.

We see this fear in another form in what is perhaps the most prominent movie about human cloning: *The Boys from Brazil*, based on Ira Levin's novel. In the 1978 film, Jewish Nazi-hunter Lieberman (modeled on Simon Wiesenthal and played by the great actor Sir Laurence Olivier) stumbles upon a plot to clone Adolf Hitler that is the brainstorm of infamous Nazi physician-experimenter Josef Mengele (who was still alive in Brazil when the movie came out). The motive of the physician-scientists here is not only amoral, but evil: to use cloning to resurrect a great, dangerous figure from the past. After all, if we could recreate dinosaurs and woolly mammoths from ancient, preserved cells, why not George Washington, ancient King Tutankhamun, or, on the dark side, Genghis Khan or Hitler himself?

Lieberman discovers that a neo-Nazi group cloned ninety-four embryos from the genes of Adolf Hitler and had ninety-four women gestate these embryos to birth. The children were then adopted by couples who matched the ages and personalities of Hitler's parents. When the little Adolfs are teenagers, their fathers fall prey to lethal "accidents" that mimic the death of young Hitler's father. Upon finally meeting one of the boys, Mengele wrongly assumes that the boy will think and feel like the real Adolf Hitler, but instead the boy is attached to his adoptive father, who Mengele has just killed. Nevertheless, the boy shows a vicious streak by allowing his Doberman Pinschers to rip Mengele apart for killing his father.

(In the movie, all the boys are identical in personality, an unrealistic result that *Orphan Black* avoids. Even with the pains the group took to match the boys with parents similar to Hitler's and ensure all experienced, like Hitler at age thirteen, the sudden death of a father who was hard to please, different parents, locales, and parenting styles would have produced different adults.)

**Fourth, people fear the motives of those who want a copy of their (or someone else's) genes to be continued in another human.** They think this is selfish, narcissistic, and doing so would result in the ancestor imposing his will on the child.

In Fay Weldon's *The Cloning of Joanna May*, nefarious sexist motives are at work when an arrogant man wants to create females who are biological replicants of his young wife, Joanna. Weldon's male protagonist creates four copies of Joanna's genotype and then implants the resulting embryos in women to be gestated. Like Henrik and his farm in *Orphan Black*, this seems to be a clear reference to compounds of polygamous Mormons in southern Utah, where elder men have a senior "first" wife and then many younger wives, some only teenagers. Only in Weldon's novel, the protagonist, through cloning, is in essence trying to recreate younger copies of his first love in order to relive previous experiences (assuming the new copies will react to him as did the first, which in reality, as we'll discuss further in later chapters, might not be true).

We see this fear most clearly in *Orphan Black* with Henrik and his use of his own sperm to fertilize Helena's eggs. Henrik is clearly a massive narcissist who not only believes himself on a mission from God, but also believes that his mission is to use biotechnology to recreate his genes with superior stock.

As we have seen already in these fictional examples, these fears certainly overlap. In real life, too, fears do not come clearly labeled in neat packages. Our fears of clones run over each other and mix with related fears about things like animal-human genetic mixes, cyborgs, and resurrected woolly mammoths.

The lasting impression of most of these notable fictional treatments is that humans originated by cloning will be exploited, treated as serfs or slaves, and never be the equal of "real" humans. Given this influence, as well as that of dozens of other novels and movies featuring cloned humans, it was understandable that, a month after Ian Wilmut announced his cloning of Dolly, he would say that human cloning would violate a right because the clone would not be treated as an individual. In all our science fiction stories, the bad guys always treat human clones unjustly. Why wouldn't we fear the real world would do the same?

Such fears tell us less about the future possibilities inherent to the existence of clones than they do about ourselves. The anxieties they express are not about cloning per se, but about how we presently relate to each other and to children.

As London psychotherapist Adam Phillips said in a symposium on human cloning, "Cloning is, for obvious and not so obvious reasons, a compelling way of talking about what goes on between people." When people worry that cloned people will be sexually enslaved or made to work in inhuman conditions in mines, they are not basing their views on evidence and reasoning but on fantasies about what they want or fear others want.

This is not unlike the teenage boy who, fed up with what he perceives as the machinations of teenage girls, says, "I just want a clone girlfriend." He doesn't want what we now know would be a human being; he wants a Stepford wife, a robot slave who will do what he wants, when he wants.

So, too, people would like an identical twin without a brain to be a source for organs when they unexpectedly get cancer or when their hearts fail with age. Who wouldn't?

As well, many of us would like a personal valet of the kind that English lords once had. Let's be honest here: When we dream of living in an ancient time, who dreams of being an illiterate serf working all day cutting wheat rather than being royalty? Who thinks that previously on the wheel of rebirth, she was once a slug?

No, we fantasize about being a superior person, one who has others at our beck and call. That is the appeal of the clone, and for many, it is a sexual appeal. The conservative political pundit Francis Fukuyama has suggested that a father would want to have sex with a clone daughter of his wife, and because the daughter is a clone and would therefore have less than human status, Fukuyama implies that the father may actually do it. In so thinking, Fukuyama seems to be saying that every father wants to have sex with his daughter, but refrains from doing so because of her normal human status. How else to explain this widespread fear, if not as an "outing" of that desire? Is that the fear in the primitive mind that sets up our "yuck" response to creating such clones?

And designer children? Simply another manifestation of how we impute bad motives to those who wish to create a child by cloning—in this case, ambitious parents rather than arrogant scientists or international biotech corporations. We fear that, given the capability, parents would only choose a very specific set of characteristics in a child—and that children so designed might be superior to the rest of us. If people didn't already see such desires in themselves and other parents, what would there be to fear?

Where does this particular fear come from? Parents often fear the influence of culture on children—for example, on young girls to sexualize themselves by wearing revealing clothing. And if our culture can do this to our daughters now, what might it do at the biological level? What if we are talking not about superficial changes but changing the underlying genes, not just for one person but for the whole continuing, biological future of a family line? The real fear is about parents' inability to resist the influence of mass culture on their kids.

And narcissists like Henrik who want to clone themselves? That fear stems from our awareness of what has always motivated people to create children, but that we rarely admit: to have something of oneself continue after death, to create a little bit of biological/genetic immortality. Or to see one's own traits flourish via their successful expression in one's children. Pride of authorship, so to speak.

But these fears about our children are not commonly discussed in private, and never in public, so we only hear about them indirectly, when we listen carefully to people talking about things such as what cloned children might be like.

## *Orphan Black* and Greek Myth

Many of the names in *Orphan Black*—Leda, Castor, and even Helena (a derivative of Helen)—derive from a famous story in Greek mythology about Leda, the queen of Sparta, and her husband, Tyndareus. According to one legend, on the same night that Tyndareus impregnated Leda, the god Zeus adopted the form of a swan and seduced (or in some versions, raped) her. Four children resulted: Helen and Polydeuces from Zeus, and Castor and Clytemnestra from Tyndareus.

Of great interest to *Orphan Black*, in some versions of this myth, Leda actually lays two eggs; Helen emerges from one and Polydeuces from the other. Since *poly* means many, *Polydeuces* could refer to several children from the same egg (like Sarah and Helena) or the same DNA (e.g., cloned children).

The choice of this myth for naming Projects Leda and Castor is apt in two other notable ways. First, critics of cloning often refer to it as "playing God," believing that humans should not be meddling in things that are the province of the divine; the choice of a story in which a god "meddles" in the affairs of humans may be intentionally ironic. Second, if we view Sarah and Helena as corresponding to the twins produced by Leda's union with Zeus, it follows—according to the narrative logic of Greek myth—that both Sarah and Helena (and Kira, because she is Sarah's daughter) might possess godlike powers, perhaps of healing.

Other objections to human cloning, those based on safety, unnaturalness, and harm to society, may actually mask religious unease. By far, the major source of all objections to human cloning is the idea that God makes babies, and that only God, not humans, should decide how and when babies come.

Consider that the most typical objections to reproductive cloning (as well as genetic enhancement) argue that "We should not play God." Other criticisms bring in God and religion by invoking human nature, with it understood that God, not human choice, created us as we are. In this sense, Ronald Nakasone, professor of Buddhist studies, University of California at Berkeley, is absolutely correct when he writes, "The cloning of human beings, like the use of artificial insemination and in vitro fertilization, is really about expanding our notion of humanity and our moral parameters."

Why, then, is cloning singled out for such special objections? The answer leaps out: There is something unique about cloning that threatens the beliefs of religious people and makes them fear it. What exactly could that be?

Father Richard A. McCormick of the Society of Jesus articulates this very well: "Viewed theologically, human beings, in their enchanting, irreplaceable uniqueness and with all their differences, are made in the image of God." McCormick and other clergy fear that cloning is a kind of secular "making" that, in the creation of the cloned baby, replaces God's hidden hand with the conscious choices of humans. (Officially, the Catholic Church only approves of creation of humans by sexual intercourse, so it opposes in vitro fertilization, which it feels also puts choice in human hands rather than God's.)

This explains part of the power of criticizing cloning as "manufacturing" human life. The implied comparison is with God's creation. Similarly, kids created by God are gifts and free, not something for which reproductive specialists need to be paid. No surprise that after thousands of years of living in societies with laws based in religious belief, our inherited ethical intuitions are steeped in assumptions about how God made the universe and wants humans to act in it.

Even if we understand genetics and how each parent contributes twenty-three chromosomes, including one sex chromosome, to the sexually created child, and even if we understand how the genetic roulette wheel mixes the genes of mother and father to create a new, unique child, we can still believe that the hidden hand of God guides the genetic mixer.

But in cloning, such belief wanes in credibility. Human beings choose to clone the genotype of a modern Leonardo da Vinci and not those of their neighbors, and that choice brings conscious human wants and decisions to the foreground. (Of course, if you believe God gave humans a brain to think and choose with, cloning doesn't threaten you at all—but such theists seem both to be in the tiny minority and uninterested in control of public policy.)

Why, I can't help wonder, should human choices about cloning be so feared and not those about, say, riding motorcycles, eating junk food, or not finishing college?

Cloning is only a tool and one that will be used by a small number of people, probably the few infertile willing to sacrifice their life's savings in trying to create a child. But people constantly confuse what they fear in themselves, or what they fear in mass culture, with fears about cloning, and so debates about cloning humans reveal more about the humans who are debating than about future humans created by cloning. When we fear sex slaves, robots, extra sources for organs, or kids who don't live up to parental expectations, we are criticizing our society, our neighbors, and ourselves. And until we can accept this, debates about cloning will never be honest.

## CHAPTER 4

# "These Crippled and Distorted Men"

## The Island of Dr. Moreau *and the Scientists of* Orphan Black

n *Orphan Black*, the key to many mysteries about the Leda and Castor siblings will presumably be found in the notes of Rachel's father, scientist Ethan Duncan, who, with his wife, Susan Duncan, originated Project Leda.

Before he kills himself—rather than allow Dyad and Topside to exploit his secret knowledge—Ethan Duncan gives Kira an illustrated copy of H. G. Wells' *The Island of Dr. Moreau*. Later, in reading to Kira, Cosima opens the book and, seeing that Duncan has scribbled between the lines and in the margins, understands that the book contains a secret message. At this point in the series, Duncan and Mrs. S. have turned over to Rachel (and Dyad) his Project Leda files on old floppy disks, but the mass of data about the DNA of the clones, especially about their synthetic DNA, is encrypted with a code that Duncan had memorized but not written down. The copy of Dr. Moreau that Duncan gifted to Kira, Cosima believes, contains a Rosetta Stone for unlocking the code.

In the same way, dear reader, the writers of *Orphan Black* give us many clues to understanding the motives and methods of its scientists by making *The Island of Dr. Moreau* so prominent in the series. It is almost as if the series is saying to us, "If you want to understand what's going on, read this book!"

Of course, *Orphan Black* contains other literary references. We are told that Helena is pursued by Dr. Aldous Leekie, who says that Helena is his "white whale," a clear reference to the equally obsessed Captain Ahab in *Moby-Dick*. Also, although *Brave New World* is not mentioned by name, references to it run throughout *Orphan Black*. Although Leekie's last name is likely a reference to the famous family of paleontologists, Louis and Mary Leakey and their equally famous scientist son, Richard (Louis' work was especially key in establishing human evolutionary development in Africa), his first name, Aldous, presumably refers to Aldous Huxley, noted author of *Brave New World*.

Interestingly, Edward Prendick, the narrator of *The Island of Dr. Moreau*, mentions that he had "spent some years at the Royal College of Science, and had done some researches in biology under Huxley." That "Huxley" would be Royal College of Surgeons professor and biologist Thomas Henry Huxley (1825–1895), notoriously known as "Darwin's bulldog" for his passionate advocacy of Darwin's views on how humans evolved from lower primates. Aldous Huxley is Thomas Henry Huxley's grandson.

Still, *The Island of Dr. Moreau* is the most conspicuous of the show's literary references. Especially in season three, we constantly hear of it and its secret message, the code that Duncan wrote around its text. But of course Duncan, and the show's writers, chose the book to begin with for good reason—another secret message. *The Island of Dr. Moreau* is a classic—probably *the* classic—book about mad scientists experimenting on humans.

Indeed, the story foreshadows many modern issues about scientists and human experimentation, which is amazing because it was published *in 1896, one hundred and twenty years ago.* It is the mother lode of Scientists Gone Wild, the tale to which all subsequent novels and movies about creating human–beast abominations, cyborgs, and all scientific things queer, weird, and yucky owe a debt.

In *The Hero with a Thousand Faces,* the noted scholar of myths Joseph Campbell taught us that, in the stories we tell, certain themes recur again and again. We try to live according to analysis and facts, but we respond to myths; narrative and story are what give meaning to our lives. In science fiction, one such iconic theme is the mad scientist—and it is *The Island of Dr. Moreau*'s prototypic version of this figure to which modern-day incarnations, *Orphan Black*'s Drs. Leekie, Nealon, and Coady included, refer.

Written by H. G. Wells, the timeless author who also wrote *The War of the Worlds*, *The Invisible Man*, and *The Time Machine*, *The Island of Dr. Moreau* tells the story of English physician-scientist Dr. Moreau, who fled London after his experiments there created scandal, and settled on a remote island in the Pacific Ocean, where he conducts experiments to transform live large mammals, such as monkeys, pigs, and leopards, into humans. Narrator Edward Prendick's suspicions are first aroused when he encounters the "crippled and distorted men" who help unload his dinghy. The men are swathed in bandages and act as if they were "jointed in the wrong place."

Then servant M'ling waits on Prendick, and Prendick notices that M'ling has Spock-like, pointed ears and eyes that glow in the dark (a prescient echo of the genetic modification of plants and fish today that can make them luminescent).

Dr. Moreau, Prendick later learns, has created a collection of half-human, half-animal creatures he calls the Beast Folk, whom he has brainwashed into accepting the Law, a code of behavior he has handed down to them (much as Henrik hands down laws for the women and men of his compound). The animal-humans are not allowed to run on all fours, eat raw flesh, or drink water with their lips to the ground. Unfortunately, the Beast Folk have an unfortunate tendency to revert to being animals.

When one of the Beast Folk, the Leopard Man, is caught hunting rabbits and eating them without cooking them, the Beast Folk hunt him down, capture him, and return him to Dr. Moreau for punishment—more hideous experiments. (In eerie anticipation of infamous Nazi physician Josef Mengele's later experiments, Moreau surgically fuses parts of animals together, the way Mengele fused identical twins together back to back. Like Mengele, Moreau is indifferent to the screams of his victims, regarding their suffering as an unfortunate by-product of his necessary experiments.) When Prendick tracks down the Leopard Man, rather than return him to Moreau's lab for more hideous experiments, Prendick—as Helena does with the Castor male Parsons in the metal halo vise—kills the Leopard Man to end his suffering.

One of the most important concepts of modern bioethics is the need for special protections from overly ambitious scientists for vulnerable research subjects. Such subjects include "captive populations" in prisons and mental institutions, cognitively challenged adults, and especially babies and children. In *Orphan Black*, as in *The Island of Dr. Moreau*, we see this need reflected in the way innocent creatures are originated in strange ways and then later studied, manipulated, and even killed for the research.

H. G. Wells saw *The Island of Dr. Moreau* as a cautionary tale about the horror of experimentation on live animals, especially without anesthesia. But over time, the novel has come to symbolize something different: first, the arrogant physician or scientist who is so obsessed by his project that he loses all ethical sense; and second, the horrors of crossing natural kinds, of mixing things that should not be mixed—of creating human cyborgs, "humanzees," and other abominations. Both these themes should sound familiar—they precisely echo two of the chief fears that arise in discussions of cloning, which we discussed in chapter three, and also appear in *Orphan Black*'s depictions of scientists.

The first theme of *Dr. Moreau* finds its purest expression in Dr. Coady, "Mother," the chain-smoking Native American scientist who oversees the clones of Project Castor (casting that brilliantly sends up stereotypes of evil white male scientists and nurturing Native American women in tune with nature). Coady believes her horrible means are justified in the name of improving humanity by ridding it of genetic diseases. Only here, *The Island of Dr. Moreau* meets *Homeland*, because big, clandestine government agencies fund her secret projects.

(Herein lies an age-old debate in applied ethics: When, if ever, does a noble end justify a horrible means? So many people justify so many terrible acts this way that you wonder if Kant wasn't right to say, "Some things are just forbidden!" One also hears Josef Stalin murmur in the background, "If you take a long enough view, *anything* is justified by the victor.")

Dr. Coady's suspension of ethics is enabled by something else she and Project Castor share in common with Dr. Moreau: privacy of location. Moreau's forbidden experiments are conducted on a rarely visited island in the Pacific Ocean, far away from the prying eyes of society. Like soldiers waterboarding alleged terrorists under orders on a tip of the island of Cuba at Guantánamo Bay Naval Station, Moreau experiments outside the legal jurisdiction of his home country, England. Similarly, in *Orphan Black*, Dr. Coady changes Project Castor for the worse in a facility in what seems to be a remote part of the Chihuahuan Desert in Mexico.

This second theme of *Dr. Moreau*, the horrors of combinations that violate nature, is one we see in a different form in another, even more famous piece of science fiction literature, named for another iconic scientist: *Frankenstein, or the Modern Prometheus*. Mary Shelley's Dr. Frankenstein—the physician-scientist who trespasses natural boundaries—and his creation still haunt us today. As in *The Island of Dr. Moreau*, we empathize with the vulnerable creatures, often persecuted and misunderstood, while recoiling against the mad scientists who violate nature. (Though, ironically, Shelley faults Dr. Frankenstein not for creating this new being but for rejecting his "son" as too grotesque and not seeing his inner moral worth.) It seems to be the destiny of the mad scientist's creation to seek its creator's love; both the Beast Folk and Dr. Coady's "sons," the Castor clones, do the same, and with as much futility. Even cold Rachel Duncan, who was created as an experiment by her father, Ethan, seeks his approval when she finally meets him. We wonder, when at the end of season three we learn that Rachel's mother, Susan Duncan, is still alive, whether Rachel will seek her love, too.

*Hubris*, in Greek mythology, is an interesting vice, a bit like the vice of pride in Christianity, but also different.

*Hubris* involves an unnatural trespass of the natural order and is often used to describe one's attempt to go beyond his or her natural place and be like the gods.

The classic example is Icarus, whose inventor father, Daedalus, makes him wings of feathers and wax. Icarus ignores his father's warning that he should fly neither too high nor too low because the Sun's heat would melt the wax and the sea's dampness would make his wings too heavy—a warning specifically phrased "be aware of your *hubris*"—and he flies too high. When the wax on his wings melts, Icarus plunges to his death.

In *Orphan Black*, as well, death is the universal price of *hubris*, and accordingly, the fate of the show's arrogant, nature-defying scientists is quite frequently death. We see this, too, in other fiction—in books and movies such as *Jurassic Park*, the scientist who clones a mammal, considered an act of scientific hubris, *must* be killed by his creation, usually in his own lab or built environment. So Ethan Duncan commits suicide in front of his clone daughter, Rachel, in an institute dedicated to advancing his work, and Aldous Leekie dies after being expelled from the Dyad Institute by his adopted daughter, Rachel. So Henrik dies in flames in his own compound at the hands of Helena, after he impregnates her with his half-clone child. So Dr. Moreau is ultimately killed wrestling with a puma on which he was experimenting.

There is one other key similarity between the scientists we see in *Orphan Black* and Wells' Dr. Moreau. Common to Drs. Moreau, Leekie, and Coady is *impatience* with the slow pace of scientific discovery and the even slower pace of evolution.

The first living cells with a nucleus emerged on Earth about two thousand million years ago. Over the next fifteen hundred million years and billions of reproductions, vertebrate animals evolved. Primates, the ancestors of humans, emerged seventy-five million years ago. It then took another sixty-three million years for the first humanlike hominins to evolve. Our species of the genus *Homo*, *Homo sapiens*, emerged a half million years ago. Some evolutionary biologists further distinguish *Homo sapiens sapiens*, a subspecies of *Homo sapiens*, emerging two hundred thousand years ago, with Neanderthal humans emerging one hundred thousand years ago. "Modern humans" emerged thirty-eight thousand years before the birth of Jesus.

The evolution of humans, in other words, took a long time. Billions upon billions of us were born and had children—some poorly adapted to harsh environments, some better adapted—and those who were able to produce the most children passed along their genes.

*Orphan Black*'s Neolutionists, the scientific organization behind Projects Leda and Castor, whose beliefs resemble those of a real-world group called *transhumanists*, champion the use of science to improve humanity. Their "self-directed" human evolution attempts to bypass the clumsy, agonizingly slow process of evolution.

Moreau would fit right in with the Neolutionists. Like them, and like the eugenics movement of the early twentieth century (which we discuss later in detail), Moreau was impatient with the pace of natural evolution and he used his experiments to see if shortcuts could be found, especially through surgery. Olivier's (surgically transplanted) tail, which Helena cuts off late in season one, perfectly fits this Moreauian nightmare.

Cloning humans, as with Dr. Moreau's experiments, allows for control that is lacking in nature. In evolution, billions of acts of creation must combine with hundreds of millions of failures to produce one exceptionally superior dairy cow or (shall we say it) Nietzsche's *Übermensch*, a superior human. But with cloning, scientists can select the exact genotype they want to recreate and then add or subtract genes to make a potentially even more superior dairy cow or human, just as Ethan Duncan added or subtracted genes to make the Ledas sterile. For Neolutionists and the rest of *Orphan Black*'s scientists, cloning presents just one more opportunity to experiment—less viscerally horrifying than Dr. Moreau's, perhaps, but, as we see in the unexpected side effects of tweaking the Ledas' and Castors' DNA, potentially as fatal.

## CHAPTER 5

# "Ipsa Scientia Potestas Est"

## The Scientific Pedigree of Cloning

To understand why we feel so strongly about human clones, you should understand the earthshaking furor that has surrounded every advance in biology over the last half century. Reproductive medicine has been especially controversial; Luddites have challenged *every* breakthrough. As you will see, it's both sad and hilarious how often the Chicken Littles of the world claim the sky is falling over even the most modest advance in helping people have children. (It's also amazing how often scientists try to become famous by faking their results.)

One of the most startling aspects of the modern science of cloning may be how everything is politicized, which is something *Orphan Black* gets right in spades. Dr. Aldous Leekie and pro-clone Rachel Duncan boast that the Dyad Corporation has lobbied Congress and the Supreme Court to create laws favoring biotechnology and their interests. Similarly, it is no accident that the main religious group opposed to cloning is the Proletheans; their name refers to pro-life movements around the world that abhor abortion and have a very expansive view of what counts as murder of a person, including a one-day-old embryo (and hence they see IUDs and morning-after pills as instruments of murder). Nor is it an accident that both the Leda Orphans and the Dyad Corporation see the Proletheans as their enemy, because the traditional Proletheans, led by Tomas (pre-Henrik), oppose both.

The Latin title of episode five of season two, "Ipsa Scientia Potestas Est," taken from the writings of scientist and philosopher Francis Bacon, loosely translates as "knowledge itself is power." Every issue in bioethics, every breakthrough in science, and every setback in medicine has a pedigree. To understand a tree in the present, you need to understand who planted the seed and the placement of its roots. This is truer of human cloning than any other issue of its kind. Likewise, to understand cloning and the public's reactions to it, as well as why Dyad and Topside are so interested in this technology, we first need a little background about assisted reproduction, the history of (and early false claims about) cloning, and stem cells. Along the way, we will also touch on some controversies that these issues introduced.

## ASSISTED REPRODUCTION

To understand cloning, you first need a little knowledge about assisted reproduction. Hard as it might be now to believe, people in the early 1970s did not distinguish between helping to create a natural child by combining sperm and an egg in a lab dish outside the womb before inserting the embryo into a woman's uterus—a form of assisted reproduction common today that has helped create millions of wanted babies—and *cloning a person* from someone else's cells. As Richard Brown, father of the first child produced by in vitro ("in glass") fertilization, said, the former is just "helping Nature along a bit"—something very different indeed from Brown cloning a copy of himself from his own cells.

After Brown's daughter Louise was born in 1978 through the work of scientists Patrick Steptoe and Robert Edwards, her birth was condemned by not one but two Nobel Prize–winning scientists: Max Perutz, who won the Nobel Prize in Chemistry in 1962 and worked at Cambridge University, and James Watson, who in 1962 shared the Nobel Prize in Physiology or Medicine for his work on DNA. Watson predicted that dangerous events would follow Louise Brown's birth. He feared that future in vitro fertilizations would lead to deformed babies who would then have to be raised by the state in custodial homes, or might even be victims of infanticide.

In all the books in which Watson has been featured, including his own famous memoir *The Double Helix*, he is shown to be arrogant, obsessed with hard science, and narcissistic. As an example, for decades Watson scorned fellow Harvard biology professor E. O. Wilson—the founder of sociobiology and a leading environmentalist—because he considered Wilson's work soft and mushy, not real science like his own. Watson also notoriously took too much credit for discovering the double helix and gave virtually no credit to fellow scientist Rosalind Franklin, toward whose work he is widely regarded as having had sexist attitudes. Perhaps surprisingly, Watson said decades later that he regretted his premature, impulsive condemnation of IVF.

## CLONING

Before Dolly the sheep was cloned, the field of cloning was rife with fraud. For example, in 1978 writer David M. Rorvik claimed in his book *In His Image: The Cloning of a Man*, that Max, a millionaire industrialist, and a host mother, Sparrow, had gestated a child from an embryo clone of Max. In 1982 a federal judge in Philadelphia ruled that his book was "a fraud and hoax."

When an egg is fertilized, its cells have the potential to become any type of cell in the body; as those cells begin dividing, the new cells differentiate, becoming liver cells or bone cells or tissue cells, to build the fetus. These undifferentiated cells are referred to as *stem cells*, first because they can regenerate themselves in a way that most cells cannot and second because all other types of cells stem from them.

Hence, they are the magic that makes cloning possible. (We'll talk further about stem cells, and their different varieties, below; see "The Definition of Cloning.")

If you looked in physiology and cell biology textbooks from 1996 or earlier, you would find a "law" of biology stating that differentiated cells could not be returned to their primordial, undifferentiated, pluripotent state. That impossibility seemed such an ironclad fact that many promising biologists had fled old-fashioned embryology for the more promising field of molecular biology (although the American ban of federal funding for research on human embryos also hurt).

Returning differentiated cells to a pluripotent state was once the Holy Grail of developmental biology because finding these stem cells in the body was extremely difficult; when they were found, they were few and hard to grow more of. If you could reverse the process of cell differentiation, then you could create gobs of pluripotent cells that could then be teased to develop any differentiated cells you required—say, to build a new liver (or a clone)—that could precisely match each patient's body and needs.

Remarkably, it was precisely that "law" about cell differentiation that Ian Wilmut—building on the work of British scientist John Gurdon and Danish scientist Steen Willadsen—overturned when creating Dolly. Back in the mid-1960s, Gurdon laid the groundwork for later stem cells and cloning research by transplanting frog-egg nuclei and, although he never used the word *clone*, creating the first functional embryo via cloning. He was followed by Willadsen, an apparently brilliant if contrarian and reclusive guy who, instead of memorizing stuff in biology textbooks, set out to prove them wrong. A Danish scientist working in Texas, he successfully created the first mammalian embryos by transferring nuclei of differentiated cells into eggs of cows in which the previous nucleus had been removed; his embryos even survived to become fetuses. However, he didn't pursue this work and was shy of publicity.

Wilmut went a step further, showing definitively that a differentiated cell from a lamb's udder could be the source of a nucleus that, inserted into an enucleated lamb egg, could produce an embryo that grew to a living, breathing adult lamb—Dolly.

---

## The Definition of Cloning

*Cloning* is an ambiguous term, even in science, and may refer to molecular cloning, cellular cloning, embryo twinning, or somatic cell nuclear transfer.

In *molecular cloning*, strings of DNA containing genes are duplicated in a host bacterium. In *cellular cloning*, copies of a cell are made, resulting in what is called a *cell line*, a very repeatable procedure in which identical copies of the original cell can be grown indefinitely. These senses of cloning match the popular sense of the term—exactly reproducing or copying a thing in an easy, repeatable way—but are not what we mean when we talk about cloning an animal or human being.

In *embryo twinning*, an embryo that has already been formed via sexual reproduction is split into two identical halves. Theoretically, this process could continue indefinitely, but in practice this twinning occurs only a limited number of times. This is also how we get identical twins.

(One thing of interest to *Orphan Black* viewers: Embryos divide and produce identical twins, as with Helena and Sarah, far more often than most people realize, meaning that many people have *ghost twins* in the womb that they never know about, which we'll talk about further in chapter thirteen. Some biologists speculate that this is because, due to limited resources, only the strongest of these twins is able to survive. Another fascinating fact about embryo twinning: Recall that Henrik discovers that Helena and Sarah, although genetically identical and both gestated in Amelia's uterus, have organs that are mirror images of each other. So if Sarah's heart is on her left, Helena's is on her right. If one is left-handed, the other will be right-handed. This is a real medical condition that happens sometimes with identical twins, called *situs inversus*.)

Finally, there is *somatic cell nuclear transfer*, a process in which the nucleus of a differentiated adult cell is implanted in an egg cell from which the nucleus has been removed. If successful, and it often is not, this creates an embryo. This is what John Gurdon and Steen Willadsen had been working on and what Ian Wilmut brought to fruition with Dolly.

Cosima uses these exact words, "somatic cell nuclear transfer, *cloning*," when she describes to Scott what Henrik did with the biological material he stole from Ethan Duncan. What biological material did Henrik steal exactly? We are not sure. But we can assume Henrik must have used a nucleus from one of his own cells, put it in an enucleated egg, and then used a surrogate mother on his farm to gestate Abel, his cloned son who dies and whose grave Sarah disturbs while a wounded Mark watches. (As we shall see in the next chapter, given the problems of getting normal primate embryos from somatic cell nuclear transfer, it is realistic that Abel died shortly after birth.)

A variant of somatic cell nuclear transfer called *fusion* describes a version of this process in which donor cells are put next to an enucleated egg and a tiny electric current is used to "fuse" the two. The electric pulse also activates egg development, and a blastocyst—a pre-embryonic cluster of about a hundred cells or less—results. (This is the type of cloning that was used to produce Dolly.)

---

## CLONING DOLLY

Before his success in 1996, Wilmut had spent years trying to clone just one lamb.

Where others had failed, Wilmut and his team succeeded in cloning Dolly by synchronizing the cell cycle phases of both the donor nucleus and recipient egg cell. During these phases, DNA starts doubling—*before* mitosis begins dividing cells to form the cell cluster that will eventually become a fetus. When other scientists had attempted nuclear transfer via fusion during this rapidly changing process, mitosis broke down, producing broken chromosomes and, consequently, mutants and defective embryos (this may be why Henrik's clone, Abel, died). So Wilmut starved egg cells to dormancy, rendering them inactive, and only then inserted a donor nucleus. In this way, he finally got mitosis to continue undisrupted, producing a healthy embryo.

While Wilmut did succeed, his methods were inefficient. He started with 277 sheep embryos, but only 29 embryos lived even a few weeks. These matured into thirteen fetuses, out of which three lambs grew to near birth size. Only one, Dolly, survived. As well, additional clones produced via his techniques have frequently suffered large-offspring syndrome, where the clones are so big that they can't be birthed normally (a condition that, in nature, can be lethal). This syndrome could be caused by nuclear transfer or by something in the uterine environment or cell culture. The lambs that died shortly after birth, unlike those that did not survive gestation, were, however, chromosomally normal.

The success of Wilmut's experiment established three important points about cloning:

1. The genes would not come from both a man and a woman but just one ancestor.
2. Accordingly, there would be no random mixing of two sets of genes, as occurs in sexual reproduction.
3. The creation of the embryo would occur, as in most forms of assisted reproduction, outside the womb in a Petri dish.

Wilmut made his claim of being the first person to have cloned a mammal from a differentiated cell cautiously, for two reasons. First, a lot scientists had been skeptical when, two decades before, Steptoe and Edwards first claimed to have created Louise Brown by in vitro fertilization, as in vitro violated similar so-called laws of nature as cloning did. Previously, several scientists had falsely claimed to have done so and had been exposed.

Second, Wilmut knew some people would not want his claims to be true, especially people such as Leon Kass, the arch-conservative bioethicist who, as we saw in chapter two, felt that cloning was against God's will, repulsive, and, above all, scary. Wilmut's success, and the specter of human cloning it introduced, galvanized Catholic and conservative Protestant theologians, who vowed not to be surprised as they had been in 1973 by the US Supreme Court's legalization of abortion; as other scientists tried to clone other mammals and as people speculated about cloning humans, they declared that here was an ethical bright line beyond which society must not trespass.

Wilmut was careful to document his claim; he had living proof of his achievement and he encouraged reporters and other scientists to visit and interact with Dolly. He also encouraged other scientists to duplicate his results.

Dolly was actually born in the summer of 1996, but Wilmut did not announce it until February 1997. Why not? Because he was also being careful about the *patents* he had filed with British authorities about various aspects of the processes he had used to create Dolly. It wasn't until his patents were approved in 1997 that he made his announcement.

## SENSATIONAL CLAIMS ABOUT CLONING

When Wilmut announced Dolly's creation and birth via cloning in 1997, many people feared that a human would soon be born the same way. Many politicians then wanted to criminalize all forms of human cloning (even animal cloning). Fortunately, this never happened.

But that was just the beginning of the furor about cloning. Shortly after Wilmut's announcement, Chicago scientist Richard Seed announced to NPR's Joe Palca that he would clone himself. Seed was not only a physicist but had also helped found a company that assisted breeders in transferring cattle embryos (the same techniques used in *Orphan Black* by Henrik Johanssen to harvest Helena's eggs and then impregnate both Helena and his daughter Gracie).

Richard Seed embodied every trope of the mad scientist. He narcissistically said he wanted to clone himself "as a step toward immortality," he didn't feel he needed anyone's permission to do so, and he seemed unaware of how his actions scared ordinary citizens. Seed's announcement about human clones being on the horizon alarmed everyone because he had expertise in the field, he had clear motives (narcissism, self-perpetuation), and, worst of all, he *looked* the part of a Hollywood-cast, elderly, creepy scientist, with his wild beard, huge head with drooping eyes, and disheveled clothes. In reality, Seed wasn't that smart and wasn't technically sophisticated in biology, so his fame soon faded—but he'd already kicked off both an international debate and paranoia about human cloning.

Next, a bizarre cult called "the Raëlians" entered the scene and claimed that it, too, would clone a child. This cult was led by Claude Vorilhon, also known as Raël, a former French racecar driver who had almost exclusively female followers living with him and with whom he liked to exercise in the nude. Add religious piety to Raël and you'd get Henrik and his rural compound with lots of young women and their children running around.

Like Henrik, Raël also had some seemingly competent female assistants, especially a biology professor and chemist named Brigitte Boisselier, who became the scientific director of Raël's company, Clonaid, which, through its mailbox in the Cayman Islands, received deposits from infertile people hoping to clone themselves or a child.

They were far from the only scammers to do this: Cypriot Panayiotis Zavos—whose PhD was in working with turkey sperm—and Italian researcher Severino Antinori also took money from clueless, infertile couples, claiming they could give the couples cloned children in their (largely fake) fertility clinics.

Throughout all this, the public had a hard time determining which claims were legitimate and which were not. The Raëlians in particular were masters of manipulating the media, and Raël and Boisselier appeared on hundreds of television programs. And why not? Every time they appeared on television, they seemed to grow in credibility and more gullible people sent Clonaid money. Even higher-ups in government were fooled. When I testified before Congress in 2001 against making human cloning a federal crime, Raël also appeared at the far end of the table.

In 2002, Clonaid falsely claimed that it had successfully cloned a human baby, whom it had named Eve. Taking it seriously, a Florida attorney asked a judge to appoint a guardian *ad litem* for Eve and threatened to sue Clonaid, because he feared it would treat Eve as a lab rat. But eventually, this attorney, the media, and everyone else realized that Raël and the rest of these claimants were just media-hungry frauds.

## REAL ADVANCES IN STEM CELLS

Although claims of human cloning proved false, there were real scientific advances taking place in a related field: stem cells.

As mentioned in the discussion of cloning earlier, stem cells are primordial, unspecialized cells that help an injured body grow new cells. For example, after blood loss, the body can activate stem cells in the blood to make new blood. In theory, stem cells could be directed to form new bones, neural cells, and cardiac tissue, and to cure sickness. This is the powerful stuff extracted from Kira's bone marrow that is being used to treat Cosima's respiratory illness.

Scientists believe that stem cells might be created using the same technique that was used to make Dolly; in fact, the original goal of Ian Wilmut and many others was not cloning, but rather finding a way to create stem cells.

But understanding what stem cells are, what they could do, their many kinds, and how to get them has taken scientists many decades. Before 1998, scientists knew that the human body *had* some stem cells (mainly in embryos or bone marrow), but they had no easy way to grow them. Then, in what *Science* magazine called "the scientific breakthrough of the year," John Gearhart of Johns Hopkins University and

James Thomson of the University of Wisconsin discovered how to make something called an immortalized stem cell line using cells originating from human embryos. Essentially, their new scientific process allowed embryonic stem cells of a particular type to be continually produced, like a little biological factory. Previously, such stem cells had to be derived, individually and tediously, from minute amounts of tissue from embryos or aborted fetuses.

## ADULT STEM CELLS DISCOVERED

In 2001, some scientists suggested that stem cells already existing in the body might be just as good for medical purposes as embryonic stem cells. Found in blood, bone marrow, and the umbilical cord, they called these *adult stem cells*, to differentiate them from *embryo-derived* stem cells. Such adult stem cells become specific kinds of cells more quickly than their embryonic predecessors. Unfortunately, most human organs contain few adult stem cells, not nearly enough to use medically; moreover, adult stem cells are even harder to grow than embryonic stem cells. Indeed, when Gearhart first investigated stem cells in the mid-1990s, he found adult stem cells so rare and difficult to extract that he decided to focus on using embryonic stem cells in his research; his production of an embryonic stem cell line was his means of assuring himself a steady supply.

The biggest benefit of adult over embryonic stem cells was political. Pro-lifers consider a human embryo to be a person, and anything that destroys such embryos is murder. Using adult stem cells in research rather than embryonic ones allowed researchers to avoid controversy.

It is adult stem cells that Sarah allows Delphine and a pediatrician to harvest from Kira's bone marrow to help Cosima in *Orphan Black*. It seems as if they are making Cosima better, and we hope they will work. In theory, they could; this isn't purely speculation. In May 2015, *USA Today* reported on the alleged recoveries of two legendary heroes of sports: National Hockey League star Gordie Howe and National Football League star John Brodie. After suffering massive strokes, both traveled outside the country for injections of stem cells from aborted human fetuses—a procedure illegal in the United States but permissible in some other places. Brodie went to Russia, Kazakhstan, and Mexico; Howe just went to Mexico. After the injections, each man's family claimed remarkable recoveries.

## PLURIPOTENT STEM CELLS

Biology progresses in fits and starts: two steps forward, one step back. Because it is so much easier to be against progress, so much easier to be a naysayer rather than a yea-sayer, and so much easier to raise alarmist ethical objections than to provide ethics cover, it is sometimes a wonder that any progress occurs in medicine at all.

Thomas Kuhn, in *The Structure of Scientific Revolutions*, proved that *paradigm shifts* move science forward, such as from the pre-Galileo belief that the Sun revolved around the Earth to the modern understanding, first forwarded by Copernicus, that the opposite is true. The cloning of Dolly was one such Copernican Revolution in biology.

Another such revolution occurred in 2007, when researcher Shinya Yamanaka of Kyoto University discovered how to use four genes to tell skin cells to revert back to pluripotent cells, or *induced pluripotent stem (IPS) cells*. In other words, Yamanaka learned how to make a differentiated, somatic cell revert back to a primordial, undifferentiated stem cell—which then could turn into anything. What this Nobel Prize–winning achievement meant, practically, was that medicine no longer required embryonic stem cells, derived from actual embryos, and no longer required eggs from female donors to create new embryos, because these powerful IPS cells eliminated the need for both. We can use IPS cells derived from our own cells as medical therapy for ourselves without the need to create, or destroy, human embryos.

## WHAT DOES THE NEAR-FUTURE HOLD?

We don't know why Topside began Projects Leda and Castor, but in the real world, cloning was only a means to an end, and that end was proving that stem cells could be manipulated to do what scientists needed to use them as the body's own medicine. This is medicine's Holy Grail. Why? Because what we all really want is (let's be honest here!) not to clone ourselves or a relative or Ian Wilmut, but to be able to use cells from our bodies to (choose one): reverse aging, heal severed spinal cords, inject new neural cells into aging brains, and, in general, to become our own individualized fountains of youth.

Anyone allowing us to do this would make billions of dollars and be awarded Nobel Prizes. On the darker side, if such stuff (or the knowledge to make it) actually existed, we can easily imagine that very rich and powerful people, especially those whose loved ones suffered terrible injuries in accidents or from hereditary diseases, might do almost anything—and pay any price—to secure such life-changing biotechnology. It would be a biological Lazarus, capable of staving off death for decades, if not raising the dead.

And we are getting oh-so-close.

As Princeton molecular biologist Lee Silver once wrote, in making fun of past naysayers: "Understanding the true nature of the gene is 'beyond the capabilities of man,' they said in 1935; it is *impossible* to determine the sequence of the complete human genome, they said in 1984; it is *impossible* to read the genetic information present in single embryonic cells, they said in 1985." Of course, all these "impossibilities" and more proved possible. With new federal funding under President Obama for the National Institutes of Health, with restrictions largely lifted on embryonic and stem cell research, and with computers assisting biologists with big data at every level, we are in a new dawn of biological revolution, which *Orphan Black* makes exciting and real.

Cloning, adult and embryonic stem cells, and the new pluripotent stem cells are all actually part of the same new explosion of interest in the nascent embryology of human life: about how changes to incredibly tiny embryos can create huge changes later on; about how to use cells of an existing person to recreate a genotype; and about how, after we are struck down by disease or accident, to tell our bodies to heal.

So let us give *Orphan Black* a little slack and accept that, somehow, Ethan and Susan Duncan, or Dyad and Topside, have, in the process of their cloning experiments, lucked into something like the biological Holy Grail of regenerative medicine in Helena and Sarah, and now Kira, too. It is an exciting premise and promises great future plots for the show.

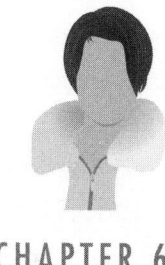

## CHAPTER 6

# What's Wrong with the Ledas?

As the last chapter shows, the history of cloning has been plagued with fraudulent claims and contested results. Every inch of progress gained has been hard won.

Nevertheless, the greatest problem today in cloning mammals is not social or political or religious objections, but the fact that, biologically and genetically, things usually go wrong in trying to create embryos healthy enough to survive to birth. This problem constitutes what could be called the Master Ethical Objection right now to creating babies by cloning from an ancestor.

The problems of creating human babies are often not appreciated until one starts trying to conceive. A woman's eggs may be the most fertile as a young teenager, shortly after menstruation begins. She then continues to be very fertile until about age twenty-eight, after which her chances of conceiving with her own eggs start to drop, such that by age forty-five her chances are low. At the same time, especially over age thirty-five, her chances of having a child with a chromosomal abnormality, such as Down syndrome, increase.

Even if a couple successfully creates an embryo, that embryo does not necessarily become a baby. Eggs are fertilized when sperm travel up a Fallopian tube to fertilize a ripe egg, after which the resulting zygote must travel down the Fallopian tube to the uterus. The uterus must then be primed with just the right mix of hormones for the embryo to attach. Later in development, there is a kind of "checkpoint" beyond which most genetically defective embryos don't pass. Exactly what this checkpoint is, is not well understood, but the fact of it is beyond doubt.

This checkpoint likely came about in human evolution to ensure that only the healthiest human embryos survive to birth. In total, about 40 percent of embryos either fail to implant on the uterine wall or miscarry, and half of those miscarried embryos and fetuses do so because of gross genetic defects.

The point is this: Even creating normal human babies is sometimes not so easy. And when assisted reproduction is needed, things get even more complicated. The reason why we have septuplets and Octomoms is that physicians sometimes put in seven or eight embryos to maximize the chance of getting one healthy, delivered child. When many or all successfully implant and grow in a womb that evolved for at most two fetuses, lack of oxygen and nutrients almost inevitably damage some of the resulting children.

Still, however hard it is to create a child through these methods, the risks and challenges in cloning as of the present are even greater—as we see even in past cloning successes and are reflected in *Orphan Black*'s Ledas and Castors. So let's look at how cloning has the potential to go wrong.

## DOLLY'S DEATH

Following Dolly's death, five months before what would have been her seventh birthday, critics claimed that there was something about her unique origination that led to her early demise—that because Dolly's DNA came from a lamb that had already lived many years, Dolly at birth had DNA whose telomeres were already short. Telomeres are the non-gene segments of DNA at the tips of chromosomes, and as they shorten, our cells age and we get age-related problems.

This controversy needs to be carefully sorted out. Every alleged fact about cloning is highly politicized and claims about how Dolly died are no exception.

Wilmut himself cites two reasons for Dolly's death. First, she was overweight, thanks to all the tourists, scientists, and reporters who fed her treats while visiting her. Second, for her protection, she lived indoors. All the time spent standing on her hind legs begging for treats, along with her extra weight, caused Dolly's hip to dislocate, which contributed to her death from a progressive, irreversible disease caused by a respiratory infection that sheep living indoors commonly contract.

However, a postmortem analysis revealed that Dolly's telomeres were in fact consistent with a lamb much older than her six years. So some reduction in her telomeres due to the advanced age of her donor's udder cells may have contributed to her death. If her immune system was weaker because her telomeres were shorter, some would argue that she had less ability to fight off the lung infection than a younger lamb.

If shortened telomeres were responsible for Dolly's death, whether directly or indirectly, this risk extends to all clones, and especially those whose ancestor was of advanced age.

## MITOCHONDRIA AND CLONING

In the previous chapter, when we outlined how originating a person by cloning differs from sexual reproduction, we said that the genes would not come from both a man and a woman but just one ancestor. That statement was made to contrast sexual reproduction with asexual reproduction (cloning)—but it was not 100 percent accurate. When the nucleus of a somatic cell is transferred from an existing person (an "ancestor"), it must be transferred *into* something, and that "something" is a healthy egg, from which the original nucleus has been removed. And it turns out that those host eggs contain some DNA.

Host eggs with their original nucleus removed still contain something called *mitochondria*, literally "grain-like threads" in ancient Greek. These threads are frequently referred to as the powerhouse of the cell; they fuel cellular processes and, when dysfunctional, can cripple the body.

More important for us, human mitochondria contain thirty-seven genes, which a clone embryo would inherit. So, given that humans have between twenty thousand and twenty-five thousand genes, it would seem the statement that a clone's genes come from just one person is *99.9 percent* correct (or, more precisely, 99.9815 percent correct).

Nevertheless, some very bad heritable diseases ride on those thirty-seven genes. So bad, in fact, that in England (but not North America), ethics committees have allowed families with devastating, inheritable mitochondrial diseases to use biotechnology to swap the bad mitochondria in the mother's egg with healthy mitochondria from a donor, in hopes of eliminating disease that may have plagued a family for generations.

Mitochondria replacement represents a different kind of gene therapy than the standard one, which fixes the lack of a particular, functional gene in a sick kid, because the changed genes are heritable and can be passed on to future generations. This is called *germ line* gene therapy (adding or replacing a single gene in a way that is not heritable is called *somatic* therapy). Although some ethicists and scientists think society should not have crossed this ethical bright line (they think somatic gene therapy is dangerous enough, let alone therapy with an impact that continues for generations), champions of germ line gene therapy retort that the whole point of making the change is to get rid of the inheritable disease *for all future children of the descendants.*

What the existence of those thirty-seven potentially deadly mitochondrial genes means for cloning is that whatever mitochondrial genes, or diseases, reside in the egg used will be inherited by any resulting clones—as well as any offspring they may produce.

## PROBLEMS WITH PRIMATE CLONING

It is an axiom of modern medical ethics that before medical experiments on humans can be considered ethical, they must first be tried on (and found nonharmful, and hopefully even beneficial, to) nonhuman animals. To be ethical, an experiment that intended to create humans by cloning would require, first, lots of evidence that scientists could one, *safely*, and two, *reliably*, clone monkeys, chimpanzees, and apes. Only after achieving those results in primates might it be permissible, in very carefully controlled circumstances, to try to originate a human by cloning. But so far cloning primates, especially those most similar to us, has not been able to produce one normal primate baby, much less produce them *reliably*.

Although many species of mammals have been successfully cloned, embryos of chimpanzees created by somatic cell nuclear transfer often have the wrong number of chromosomes and therefore do not implant properly in the host uterus. After the primate embryos were created, their cells did not seem to divide properly.

In cell division, or mitosis, the replication and division of chromosomes is guided by things called *spindles*. Two key proteins (NuMA and HSET) guide the organization of other proteins necessary for the development of the embryo. In primates, these *spindle proteins* concentrate near the chromosomes of unfertilized egg cells—the same chromosomes that are removed to make way for the new adult cell nucleus in somatic cell nuclear transfer. The process of removing the old nucleus and inserting a new nucleus seems to damage spindle proteins. In non-primate mammals, these proteins appear throughout the egg cell, making it easier to replace the nucleus by cloning without damaging them.

To find out what went wrong in cloned monkey embryos, a team at the University of Pittsburgh School of Medicine fluorescently labeled the parts active during division of cells. They discovered that the *mitotic* (as in mitosis) *spindles* that guide chromosomes in cell division did not function correctly in cloned embryos. More important, they found that either the cloned monkey embryos lacked the NuMA and HSET spindle proteins or the two proteins were not functioning properly. Getting primate embryos (and therefore human embryos) to have these two key proteins, and to then have those proteins function correctly in organizing chromosomes around spindles, may be the key to successful human cloning. Recall that Ethan Duncan brags to Cosima in season two, episode six, that he and his wife, Susan, had "solved the spindle problem." This is exactly what he is talking about.

In 2007, a team of researchers at Oregon Health & Science University did successfully create a stem cell line from a cloned primate nucleus. They also used somatic cell nuclear transfer, but did so more precisely. They didn't use the DNA stains and X-ray lighting they had used previously, because they believed these techniques were what had harmed the primate's DNA. Instead, they used a machine called "Oosight," which allowed them to see the DNA-carrying structures in the egg. Importantly, the researchers micro-surgically gathered chromosomes at the right time during embryo formation so that the spindle proteins needed for each chromosome were present and functioning correctly. So they *were* able to successfully clone primate fetuses.

As Ethan Duncan would say—they solved the spindle problem! At least, they would have solved it, if they had been able to show that the babies that resulted would not miscarry and, when born, would be healthy and normal. We don't know exactly why, but none of the primate fetuses completed gestation to birth. The Oregon team transferred seventy-seven embryos into different surrogates, but no fetus made it to day twenty-five.

One problem is that, to produce a viable fetus, the cycle of the cloned embryo has to *perfectly* match the menstrual cycle of the surrogate mother, a very difficult task to accomplish. Another problem lies within the embryonic cells themselves: They do not have the right epigenetic programming— supra-genetic instructions that affect gene function—to mature into an actual monkey. Cloned embryonic cells may lack the signals that would turn key genes on, or off, at various stages in gestation. So any resulting primate babies almost certainly are going to be born with major defects, such as the Leda girl Charlotte's leg problems in *Orphan Black*.

It's worth noting that the same team from Oregon Health & Science University also created human embryonic stem cells using the techniques, but the university's Institutional Review Board (IRB) and Ethics Committee blocked them from creating human embryos this way. This recalls Ethan Duncan's comment that his "Ethical Oversight Committee" regarded his work creating viable, cloned human embryos as "an ethical failure." The reasoning for the committee's judgment in the show is not clear, though one would hope that it didn't just beg the question and assume that any creation of healthy human embryos by cloning was inherently wrong. (Nor do we know exactly what kind of ethics oversight committee it was. If in America, it would either be an IRB—for research funded with federal funds—or an internal ethics committee of a corporation such as at Merck or Monsanto. England and Canada have similar committees with different names and slightly different mandates.)

Why might this otherwise be an ethical issue? When fetuses don't have the proper genes turned on or off at the right times, or don't have the proper number of chromosomes, they will be born with significant problems. For instance, Down syndrome is due to a chromosomal abnormality; so is Turner syndrome in females, as well as Klinefelter syndrome.

Thus, any experiment that cloned human embryos from an ancestor and implanted them in the wombs of real women would run a high risk of creating babies with chromosomal defects, as well as other defects caused by genes not turning on or off at the right times in gestation.

As previously noted, this is the major reason why originating babies by cloning is unethical. There is a very high likelihood that any babies so produced would have major structural abnormalities, problems caused by deep-down irregularities in their genes and cells. As there are many other ways to create human babies, by sex or assisted reproduction, and many other ways to get children, using surrogates or by adoption, there is now no cogent ethical argument for allowing experiments to create human children by cloning.

## WHAT'S WRONG WITH THE LEDAS?

In *Orphan Black*, a lot of things went wrong with clones: The Castor males have a brain disease; several of the Ledas, including Cosima, suffer (or suffered, in the cases of Jennifer, Katja, and another unknown clone from Poland) from fatal or potentially fatal autoimmune respiratory diseases; Charlotte has a condition that causes her leg not to function correctly, possibly of neurological origin.

Exactly what is wrong with the Ledas is hard to determine. We know that the Ledas are supposed to be sterile, but that Sarah is not. We know that high school teacher Jennifer, the German Leda Katja, and the Polish clone suffered from a respiratory/lung illness that killed them. We see Katja spitting up blood. We know Jennifer's last days were spent at the Dyad Institute, which wasn't able to prevent her early death.

There are several possibilities here. First, inheriting shortened telomeres from Kendall Malone, who was already middle aged when her cells were used, may be to blame; their immune systems might not be as healthy as a normal young woman's.

Second, there might have been something in the mitochondria of egg donors that causes these issues. We know that Amelia was a surrogate mother for both Helena and Sarah, but probably the eggs that were used came from other, younger women; young eggs work best, and creating embryos from eggs other than those of the surrogates would give experimenters more control over the whole process. Almost certainly, each of the other Ledas would have come from a different egg; each egg may have come from a different woman and so could have different mitochondrial genes. That would help explain why some of the Ledas are affected and others are not.

Third, something might have gone wrong in the chromosomal reassembly of certain Ledas (like the problems with primates) that affects their lungs and maybe every cell in their bodies.

Fourth, something could have gone wrong with the attempt to make the Ledas sterile. This seems to be the main hypothesis the show suggests. Cosima tells Delphine and Scott that the polyps in Jennifer's lungs and uterus seem to be from *an autoimmune disease*. Ethan Duncan says as much to Cosima, with the added regret that "we didn't foresee the consequences" of using that method to cause sterility, meaning he didn't foresee that it might also cause illness and/or early death.

Kira's miraculous stem cells helped Cosima, presumably by pumping up her immune system to ward off the bioengineered polyps growing inside her lungs and uterus (evidence that shortened telomeres, and the attendant immune issues, are to blame). Whether Kira's stem cells would also help the Castors is unclear.

## WHAT'S WRONG WITH THE CASTORS?

The Castors' autoimmune problems could result from shortened telomeres, as well, but issues with their mitochondria present a more likely answer.

Mitochondrial diseases can be really devastating; they resemble fatal neurological diseases, with symptoms similar to Alzheimer's, Parkinson's, muscular dystrophy, amyotrophic lateral sclerosis (Lou Gehrig's disease), and other terrible, degenerative neuromuscular diseases. When mitochondria become dysfunctional or start to die, this disease process affects every cell in the body. Given the way that mitochondrial diseases manifest, it is very likely that the Castors, either by design or, more likely, by error, have a defect in their mitochondria.

Remember when Scott autopsies the brain of killed Castor clone Seth? Scott examines Seth's brain tissue under a microscope and exclaims to Cosima, "It's like Swiss cheese, with amyloid plagues and rapid cell death. He wouldn't have lived a week." To which Cosima says, "It's like Creutzfeldt-Jakob disease."

Creutzfeldt-Jakob disease (CJD) is a spongiform encephalopathy, a type of disease that makes the brain swell to bursting while destroying its tissue and leaving spongelike holes. If you think that this disease class is rare or impossible, think again. Most recently, a 2015 issue of the *New England Journal of Medicine* reported the deaths from a deadly new viral encephalopathy of three Germans who bred squirrels (the virus presumably jumped species somehow).

CJD has a fascinating backstory. German neurologists Hans Gerhard Creutzfeldt and Alfons Maria Jakob first published reports around 1920 of the fatal encephalopathy in humans that now bears their names. In 1976, D. Carleton Gajdusek shared a Nobel Prize with Baruch Blumberg for proving that CJD could be transmitted via brain tissue from one person to another (which, given the close resemblance of the Castors to victims of CJD, could suggest that the Castors were infected by scientists experimenting on them, rather than their disease being mitochondrial). In fact, CJD and other spongiform encephalopathies can be transmitted in various ways: by a virus, by injecting brain tissue of one animal into another, and possibly by eating the dead remains of infected animals. Between 1956 and 1984, some infertile women and very short children received hormones from pituitary glands of human cadavers to treat their infertility and growth issues, respectively. About 1985 (when authorities forbade further injection of such hormones), after many women had strangely died, scientists learned by autopsy that some of these women and also many British adults who had been given the hormones had died young from CJD from the infected hormones.

In 1997, pioneering scientist Stanley Prusiner received a Nobel Prize in Physiology or Medicine for proving, despite decades of skepticism of his colleagues, that a new class of self-reproducing pathogens associated with proteins could transmit lethal encephalopathies. Such proteins, called *prions*, probably cause CJD and other spongiform encephalopathies to be transmitted from one animal to another and, importantly, are not killed by standard methods of preventing infection, such as boiling or heating over flames.

All the encephalopathies are fatal; after symptoms appear, they lead to death in a few years or less. So what afflicts the Castors is very serious stuff. If it resulted from some mysterious contamination in their origination by cloning, that is a very bad thing. If it was built into them by design, that's pure evil. That would mean the military clones had been programmed to die as young men.

The most well known of the encephalopathies is Mad Cow Disease, a bovine spongiform encephalopathy (BSE) that was discovered in 1986 to have infected hundreds of thousands of British cattle. In the 1990s, about forty people in England died from Mad Cow Disease. The disease is incurable and from signs of its first symptoms, it takes about fifteen months to kill. It appears that these people did not contract BSE from the infected cows directly, but rather contracted a form of CJD by eating meat from cows fed the remains of BSE-infected sheep. Because the disease may take decades to develop, and can only be verified with a brain autopsy, for which most families refuse to pay, exact figures for Mad Cow deaths are hard to determine. But the autopsies that were performed found infectious prions in victims' brains, meaning it is almost certainly true that these BSE-causing prions were transmitted from infected meat to the human who consumed it. Alarmingly, cooking the meat did not stop the transmission.

We know that viruses also transmit BSEs, and now we know that prions transmit BSEs in ways hard to stop. So it is therefore possible that a Castor might spread a spongiform encephalopathy to female partners through intimate sexual contact.

In *Orphan Black,* we learn from the physician at the desert military compound that Dr. Coady's original project was to cure the Castor men of their degenerative problem. But then, the physician tells Paul Dierden, Beth's original monitor and a major in charge of the Castors, that a Castor brought back an infected woman, whom Dr. Coady studied. After that, the doctor says, Dr. Coady changed the nature of the research project—from saving the lives of his Castor brothers to something more sinister, involving, as Paul later puts it, "unsanctioned experiments on civilians," in particular deliberately infecting unsuspecting women with a lethal disease. Dr. Coady told the Castor men to start keeping logs of the women with whom they had sex and to log a sample of their hair (for their DNA).

Toward the end of season three, Dr. Coady tells Paul that "Castors and Ledas have the same defect. It attacks the boys' brains and the women's epithelial tissue." Dr. Coady wants Sarah because she believes Sarah can fight off the infection, a hypothesis Coady proves when she drugs Sarah and transfuses her with two units of Rudy's blood. Sarah gets feverish and sick but quickly recovers. Still, whether Dr. Coady is correct about the Ledas and Castors having the same disease remains to be seen; Sarah's lack of sterility and her ability to fight off the Castor infection are not necessarily related.

The show does offer one piece of evidence that they are, however: By comparing blood from a sick Gracie and cells from Seth's brain autopsy, Delphine helps Cosima and Scott discover that both share a "weird protein," made to look like an orange mini-monster on the computer screen. This weird protein—possibly a prion—is what has been making the Castor males sick and what they have been spreading sexually to unsuspecting women. The show suggests this may be the cause of sterility both in the Ledas and in the Castor males' sexual partners.

## ORPHAN BLACK AND DARK SCIENCE

One of the best things about *Orphan Black* is how often it gets the science right. However, not all the science in *Orphan Black* is correct, and the Castor clones' likely spongiform encephalopathy is one example that doesn't check out.

During the sixth episode of season three, "Certain Agony of the Battlefield," things get a little harder to understand. After being told by the physician that Dr. Coady's research project on the Castors changed when a Castor brought back an infected woman, Paul blurts out, "It's a weapon!" Dr. Coady seems to agree. And it is possible that an infectious protein spread sexually could be a "weapon," say, to sterilize women—especially if one goes with the paranoid thought, held by some in the early days of AIDS, that HIV was created to wipe out gay men and promiscuous black people.

But Dr. Coady goes on to defend herself by claiming that, "It could end all war. In a single generation." It is unclear how something spread sexually could "end all war." Then she adds another, seemingly different claim: "The science in that room could change the very nature of humanity." How that is so also remains unclear.

Of course, other weird stuff has happened in *Orphan Black* that takes us beyond plausible science—the possibly miraculous healing powers of the stem cells of Sarah, Helena, and especially Kira, for one.

Pluripotent stem cells could one day be wondrous and nearly miraculous, as we discussed last chapter. Henrik is right, in season two, to regard biotechnology as something both life changing and humanity changing. Stem cells could even be seen, religiously, as God's gift to humanity, a biological treasure whereby a person's own cells are turned into healing machines to cure his or her sick or injured body. Many people, including this author, have championed a new era of "regenerative medicine" and "personalized genomics" based on use of a patient's own stem cells. But the FDA has yet to approve stem cell treatments in anything but experiments, and those experiments have failed to uniformly prove great results. Unfortunately, unlicensed American clinics offering therapies based on stem cells (which can operate due to a loophole in FDA regulations), or even more unregulated clinics in Mexico and abroad, prey on those impatient with the slow pace of approval, charging exorbitant fees to gullible patients.

Even taking into account stem cells' future potential, Kira's nearly instantaneous healing in the emergency room after being hit by a car, and Helena's recovery after Sarah shoots her, border on the scientifically unbelievable. It is just not in the realm of possibility and starts to creep over the line into the supernatural.

Two other incidents in *Orphan Black* cross that line and call for explanation. First, there is Olivier's tail (which Helena, fascinated by it and considering Olivier an abomination, cuts off), and second, that wormlike thing in Dr. Nealon's mouth that seems to attack Delphine in the final episode of season three.

In the unlikely event that it were possible to make such biological changes, for example, by genetic tampering with the embyro, they would be somatic changes, not germ-line changes. That is, they would modify the existing genes of a person but would not change his or her germ-line cells and so not be passed on to future generations through sexual reproduction. Even if Neolutionists used cloning to create an embryo with such characteristics (as cloning would give scientists the chance to *choose* the particular nucleus inserted into the egg and, more important, to modify it there), there is still that checkpoint in human embryonic gestation that genetically defective embryos generally don't pass. Any embryo with a tail or wormlike tongue would not make it past this checkpoint and, hence, would not be born. And this is not even getting into the medical problem of the immune system, which rejects any kind of foreign tissue, and a wormlike appendage or tail is about as foreign as you can get.

## ONGOING MYSTERIES

What is wrong with the Ledas is an ongoing mystery in *Orphan Black.* Their physical ailments create both problems for the Ledas and a sense of urgency to find a cure. What the eventual cure turns out to be, should they find one, could point to the inherent biological problems of being originated by cloning, or the quite different problems of bioengineered cloned humans being sterile, "weapons," or something else. Both have a strong scientific basis, but each suggests a different set of ethical questions for the show to explore.

CHAPTER 7

# The Ethics of Synthetic Biology

In 2010, one of the most well-known scientists and entrepreneurs on the planet made international news in announcing his creation of a "synthetic organism." Craig Venter, already famous for beating the United States government's Human Genome Project in the race to sequence the human genome, had already founded the for-profit gene company Celera Genomics in 1998.

Celera, which in 2011 became a subsidiary of Quest Diagnostics, sounds a lot like the Dyad Corporation (which, similarly, appears to be a subsidiary of shadow corporation Topside) in *Orphan Black*. From top to bottom, Celera and

Quest aim to make money from knowledge of genomics, especially the new medical field of personalized genomics, where diagnosis and treatment are tailored to your individual genetic profile (presumably a specificity for which you or your insurance company is willing to pay).

Venter also founded The Institute for Genomic Research (TIGR), a nonprofit think tank employing more than four hundred people who analyze ethical and policy implications of genetic research. This sounds a little like Harry H. Laughlin's nonprofit Station for Experimental Evolution, which championed the notorious eugenics movement in North America in the early twentieth century (more about this in chapter eight), especially since it is hard to believe that the profit-minded Venter would fund analyses of policies that could hurt Celera or Quest.

Now, in 2010, Venter claimed to have made something that had never existed before in nature: a completely artificial, or rather synthetic, cell, which he named "Synthia." Rather than being inherited from a previously living cell, the cell's DNA code was created by Venter. Venter's work has a way of grabbing everyone's attention, and his announcement that he had created Synthia led many to wonder if this wasn't another biological boundary crossing.

The term *synthetic biology*, or *SynBio*, can refer to everything from putting a new gene into a potato to creating biological life out of chemicals; the exact definition is up for debate. But for our purposes, we will use the phrase to mean the deliberate introduction of genes to create life forms that did not naturally arise through evolution.

Under this definition, the Ledas and Castors are instances of SynBio.

## FOUR FRAMES FOR THINKING ABOUT BIOTECHNOLOGY

Ethics around SynBio are just as contested as the term's precise definition. But there are four philosophical frames that can help us think more clearly about SynBio's ethical implications, in *Orphan Black* and in general: *naturalism*, *globalism*, *transhumanism*, and *egalitarianism*.

A frame in the philosophical sense is a specific viewpoint that dictates the way one thinks about a subject or the kind of questions one asks. Using frames allows us to understand particular ethical issues in their larger, sometimes opposing, contexts. Frames can also help us understand where, philosophically, some of the characters in *Orphan Black* are coming from.

*Naturalists* such as the Prolethean Gracie believe that human societies have strayed too far from traditional forms of living. They cherish environmental purity and yearn to leave Earth as our forefathers inherited it. They believe biological engineering should be resisted, especially if it violates natural norms, creates strange hybrids, and upsets Mother Nature. Naturalists want to keep humanity pure. They fear *Jurassic Park* and oppose bringing back woolly mammoths. To naturalists, the Ledas and Castors are unnatural freaks, things that should be abhorred.

*Globalists* such as (we assume) the executives of Topside and the Dyad Institute believe that a rising sea lifts all boats. Strong economies, not moral passion, raise standards of living. In the long run, free world trade, specialization, investment of capital, and economies of scale help more people than international aid. They believe that protecting breakthroughs in biotech with patents will motivate scientists to create things that benefit everyone, the way Apple and Google have. To ensure fairness, countries must enforce laws about intellectual property and not allow people to steal from other countries.

Naturalist Gracie would despise the globalist attitude of turning nature into private property. According to real-life naturalist and activist Vandana Shiva, "The patenting and ownership of life forms is ethically [wrong] . . . When a pig or cow is simply treated as bioreactor, for instance, to produce a certain kind of chemical for the pharmaceutical industry, it can be re-engineered and redesigned without any ethical constraint."

*Transhumanists* such as Dr. Aldous Leekie believe that science can solve all human problems and that biotechnology not only can, but has a duty to, improve human life, both by eliminating inherited diseases and by creating better people. For them, genetic engineering creates safer medicines, healthier foods, and cures for infertility. Science will ultimately solve all problems if Luddites such as Tomas can be overcome. For transhumanists, a tool is a tool is a tool, and it is the people who use them that are good or bad. Cloning, whether of humans or mammoths, is a tool and can be used for good or evil purposes just like a hammer or a gun. Topside and Dyad seem to have bad motives for cloning Ledas and Castors, but other people could have good motives.

For example, Venter, the ultimate transhumanist, believes that Synthia could help cure diseases and feed the planet, though naturalist and egalitarian critics doubt that, even if he has really created a totally artificial living cell, its use will benefit most people rather than rich corporations investing in biotech. Naturalists also argue that Synthia is dangerous, because it has qualities that did not develop, as every other kind of cell did, via evolution, and hence have not been tested by Nature.

*Egalitarians* such as Kira's father, Cal Morrison, believe that the world's problem is not lack of scientific knowledge, but injustice. For Cal and other egalitarians, everything about patenting life forms, whether a genetically modified tomato, a cloned cat, or a Leda with a patent tag, favors organizations like Topside and Dyad—in other words, Big Pharma, Big Biotech, and the top 1 percent.

Cal would dismiss the claims that markets naturally lift everyone in a rising sea or that biotechnology will help the average person. Rather, egalitarians believe corporations such as Monsanto will use biotechnology to maximize profits and exploit the poor. Biotech will make the world more unequal, not less. For example, Monsanto genetically modifies plants for herbicide resistance. This concentrates Monsanto's control of agriculture because crops that remain vulnerable to the herbicides cannot be grown in fields nearby Monsanto's.

## EXAMPLES OF SYNTHETIC BIOLOGY AS SEEN THROUGH THE FOUR FRAMES

Since 2010, synthetic biology has exploded, worrying naturalists and egalitarians.

For example, scientists have genetically modified pigs to produce manure with less phosphorus, a chemical whose release into waterways causes algae to bloom and clog the surface. But to make pigs produce less environmentally damaging manure, scientists had to insert genes from a mouse and the *E. coli* bacteria into pig embryos, creating what some naturalists call "Frankenswine." To naturalists, this was a border crossing, a violation of the natural.

Scientists' efforts to raise pigs with less harm to the environment are ostensibly something naturalists would like, except that naturalists also oppose the gigantic pig factories that create the problem—an unethical, unnatural way of raising pigs, versus raising them free range—and hence oppose solutions that make it easier to keep those factories in business. Similarly, naturalists oppose Frozen Zoo, a nonprofit project that freezes embryos of endangered species for later possible implantation. Naturalists prefer to focus on preventing loss of habitat rather than high-tech solutions to loss of species due to habitat destruction.

In Canada, scientists genetically altered dairy cows to be 75 percent less gaseous, drastically reducing the methane gas that contributes to global warning. And as with the gene-altered pigs, you would think naturalists would like this, but again, they do not, because they favor organic dairies, milk without added hormones, and genetically unmodified cows over industrial dairy farming.

Of course, egalitarians oppose the alterations to both types of livestock, because they believe such changes make it easier for Big Agribusiness to treat animals like commodities.

Another biotech company, Nexia Biotechnologies, inserted into the DNA of goats a gene responsible for making web material in spiders, resulting in bioengineered milk with proteins that can be turned into amazingly strong fibers called "BioSteel." For egalitarians, this was another example of scientists plundering nature for profits, the way Shaman Pharmaceuticals controversially sent anthropologists in the late 1990s to cozy up to shamans in South America to steal and patent their secret plants and cures.

Similarly, AquaBounty, a for-profit genetics company, genetically modified salmon to grow twice as fast as normal. Naturalists opposed the release of such salmon into the wild, worried that the genetically modified salmon would drive out natural salmon, but the FDA approved sales of such fish in 2015.

Researchers have also inserted small bits of hepatitis B and cholera genes into bananas, so that the people in developing countries eating these bananas can be easily vaccinated. But that project has gone nowhere—and egalitarians would argue that's because no one can discover how to make money doing it.

As a last example, scientists in Washington State genetically engineered poplar trees to have roots that soaked up 90 percent of environmental trichloroethylene, a toxic chemical found in the soil of hazardous waste sites, beating ordinary poplars, which absorb only 3 percent. Of course, they patented these GM poplars and hope to make big money selling them to the federal government to clean up these sites.

## SYNTHETIC BIOLOGY AND *ORPHAN BLACK*

So what does all this mean for *Orphan Black*?

In the show's science fiction world, Projects Leda and Castor scientists seem to have used some synthetic biology in the human clones, especially for their DNA tags and maybe other things we don't yet know about. Indeed, this revolutionary technology probably explains the extraordinary healing qualities of Kira, Helena, and Sarah. We see in Aldous Leekie how transhumanists think that the new technology sketched in the show might have good uses.

Naturalists see things differently. In all her natural innocence, Gracie is powerfully repulsed by the idea of clones, feeling that Helena is an abomination, and is shocked by the discovery that her husband, too, was a creation of science. Her ideas reflect our innate sense of wrongness about humans meddling with nature, genes, and the very things that make us human.

Naturalists and egalitarians both worry about risks to the health of those working with synthetic organisms. Biocontainment is not a certain science. Also, organisms that escape or are deliberately released into the environment or into a human subject could wreak havoc if not properly oryrtffortcontrolled. The most serious fear of naturalists and egalitarians is that synthetic biology might provide powerful but unpredictable new tools for making living organisms into biological weapons.

In *Orphan Black*, the Castors portray both concerns. They are controlled by the military, having been trained as soldiers as a kind of biological weapon. But what is scarier is the information revealed about their condition—that their strange disease is transmissible. Under Coady's fearsome control, there is, as Paul suggests, the possibility that the Castors' disease could, in fact, be a bio-weapon. What if Dyad created a new batch of human clones—call them Victors—and infected them with the lethal virus of the film *Contagion*, then blackmailed the world to prevent the Victors' release into the general population?

Egalitarians are of course also concerned with whether, if SynBio essentially manipulates the genetics of organisms for specific purposes, the development of such technology will promote just or unjust distributions of power and resources. The most basic research with SynBio raises questions about justice for those involved—not only for those who work in labs creating SynBio, but also anyone in a medical trial as a research subject. The Ledas and Castors are *unconsenting* subjects to their experimental origins and *unconsenting* subjects of the ongoing monitoring of their lives.

There are also justice concerns about the downstream consequences of SynBio. Louisiana's Chemical Corridor, an eighty-five-mile stretch from New Orleans to Baton

85

Rouge, is famous for the environmental harm of its many chemical plants and oil refineries. It's also called the Cancer Corridor due to its demonstrated effects on its residents. Most of the people who live here are poor and black—an example of *environmental racism*, which occurs when one racial group disproportionally suffers harm from such environmental conditions.

Will SynBio lead to a similar "biological racism"? Will poor people, and especially poor minorities, be left out of, say, the race for biologically superior children through genetic engineering? Will "equality of opportunity" become the opportunity of biologically "normal" children to line up at the starting line of life, only to be quickly left behind by newly created Superior Children?

SynBio might also lead to the elimination of the means of livelihood of people in developing countries. Before relations thawed with America, every Cuban village had a public phone and a person who made a living relaying messages from that phone. Now new cell phone towers are being built, allowing everyone to have an affordable cell phone, but destroying a major occupation in Cuba. In the same way, huge monocrops of soybeans, corn, and rice are destroying family farms around the world, rendering them obsolete and inefficient.

One concern very apparent in *Orphan Black* centers on the ownership of and control over SynBio. With patents embedded into their very DNA, the clones of Castor and Leda are, to Topside at least, mere biological possessions—investments to be traded on commodity exchanges or used as weapons by the military.

Egalitarians worry about Big Pharma—corporations—being able to dictate the terms of use for SynBio, much as Dyad and Topside, as owners of the patents on the Ledas' (and maybe the Castors') DNA and the only ones monitoring them, control the medical information gleaned from the clones. And as we will see later in discussing patents, many companies have tried to control all the new genetic knowledge they acquired to maximize profits, and do not generally, or freely, share that knowledge with other companies.

## SYNBIO AND JUSTICE IN THE REAL WORLD

In our world, things with SynBio overall are actually even more alarming than *Orphan Black* portrays, and certainly more than most people realize. Scenarios that used to be science fiction are now reality. A 2015 issue of *WIRED* magazine headlined the "Genesis Engine," another name for CRISPR, a cheap, efficient, patented gene-editing method that lets almost any geneticist insert new genes into old organisms, allowing each to potentially change our natural world. With CRISPR, almost anyone with moderate training in genetics can do "garage bio" or "DIY bio," so it will be almost impossible to regulate or control what genes are put into what organism.

New genetic sequencers have allowed scientists, within a decade, to jump from analyzing a billion base pairs per run to eighteen trillion base pairs per run. Nicknamed "Wonder Woman," "Batman," and "Electra," these super-sequencers at places such as the HudsonAlpha Institute for Biotechnology in tech-centric Huntsville, Alabama, also allow analysis, cell by cell, of what is occurring in the brain or immune system.

New biotechnology that uses such sequencers and CRISPR will affect the lives of billions of people, people who are unlikely to have a voice in decisions about which genes are inserted into what organisms and why, but who will disproportionately experience the impact of any disasters. A fundamental principle of justice is at stake here: When scientists experiment with the foundations of life in ways that potentially harm or benefit billions of people, how do we ensure a just outcome? The globalist perspective seems to leave 99 percent of people behind, with organizations like Topside in control.

The key to preventing this in our world is discussion among scientists themselves about how much technology like CRISPR should be allowed to be developed and used, rules around sharing results from that technology freely with journalists and citizens, and possible regulation by government agencies such as the FDA and the National Institutes of Health.

As for *Orphan Black*, it is important for experts outside the corrupt world of Dyad and Topside to have a look into the dealings of Projects Leda and Castor. Only through this can the clone sisters and brothers hope for salvation from the constant manipulation and objectification to which they are subject. Only in this way can the other 99 percent have a say in the future of humanity and the planet.

## CHAPTER 8

# Orphan Black and the Ethics of Patenting Human Life

I ntellectual property relating to biotechnology is one of the most exciting and also one of the most complicated areas of modern law, encompassing state, federal, and international statutes, as well as dozens of agencies such as the NIH, FDA, and State Department issuing regulations short of laws that still govern scientists. The best law students at Stanford and Yale work mightily to try to understand these issues and discover just solutions—no easy task, for them or us.

Early on in *Orphan Black,* we learn two amazing things: first, that each sestra clone's DNA includes a unique "tag" by which she can be identified; and second, that these tags are patented by the Dyad Institute, or perhaps Topside.

Is this science fiction or real science? What exactly is a DNA tag? And can it be patented?

## DNA TAGS

DNA tags—or more accurately, *expressed sequence tags* (ESTs)—mark short sequences of much longer strands of DNA and are used to easily identify such longer sequences for legal and scientific purposes. Although not an exact analogy, ESTs are a bit like emblems on automobiles made by Mercedes, Toyota, or Nissan that clearly show the manufacturer.

Human DNA is made up of three billion base pairs. We have 23 pairs of chromosomes, each varying in length between 750,000 and 250 million base pairs. Our 140,000 genes—sequences of DNA that can vary in length between 781 and 2 million base pairs—don't make up a huge percentage of those base pairs, but they govern many aspects about us by directing cells' production of the proteins that are used to regulate our biological functions.

Using enzymes, it is possible to find markers for the DNA sequences that control specific proteins—these markers are ESTs. Controversial entrepreneur Craig Venter, the pioneer of synthetic biology I mentioned in the previous chapter, was also the leader in identifying such ESTs, using powerful computers on behalf of the NIH. (Venter has replaced James Watson as the most visible molecular biologist in North America and, maybe, the world.)

Why are ESTs useful? A list of ESTs provides a template for individual genes' locations in our DNA, allowing scientists to experiment and discover what functions each gene, or batches of genes, might control.

So given that the sestras are originated by cloning, and so had some scientist could have tinkered with their individual copies of Kendall Malone's genome, it would be possible to use a unique DNA tag to identify them. Whether that tag could, or should, be patentable is another question.

## PATENTING LIFE

Historically, US patent law does not allow patents on naturally occurring things such as rocks, plants, and chemical elements. However, in *Diamond v. Chakrabarty* (1980), the US Supreme Court ruled that geneticist Ananda Chakrabarty could patent a genetically modified organism designed to clean up oil spills. The Court said that because Chakrabarty had changed the genes of a preexisting organism, the new organism became a "human-made invention," not something occurring wild in nature, and therefore could be patented.

A year later, in the *In re Bergy* case (1981), a lower court explicitly, and controversially, emphasized that "the fact that microorganisms . . . are alive is a distinction without legal significance." Critics immediately complained that *Bergy* treated life as "an industrial tool," not as something sacred, and claimed that "life itself, even at its lowliest, is invested with a sanctity that the patent process defiles." They saw *Chakrabarty* as championing the worldview that nature is something to be owned and manipulated.

About a decade later, Craig Venter, who was at the time working to locate and mark genes for the NIH, tried to get the agency to patent his discoveries. The NIH submitted an application, but due to criticisms from both academic researchers and religious groups about patenting life, the Patent and Trademark Office rejected NIH's application, and in 1994, NIH withdrew it. (Venter himself left NIH shortly after its initial application in 1991 to continue to search for DNA tags as part of his nonprofit, TIGR, as mentioned. He also formed its for-profit partner, Human Genome Sciences, which notably beat NIH in sequencing the human genome. Its backing came from venture capitalists hoping to profit from drugs and proteins developed from TIGR's knowledge.)

Despite the NIH's application not resulting in any patents, the three-year process sparked controversy. It also spurred private companies to apply for patents on their own DNA tags and other gene sequences—some of which were granted in a very liberal interpretation of existing laws (a problem we'll discuss later in this chapter).

Most important, controversial, and bizarre of all, applications proceeded for patents on DNA tags covering large sections of human DNA where researchers had no idea what was going on—whether the proteins regulated by these bits of DNA did a lot or did nothing. In short, patents were being granted even though the holder of the patent didn't know what his "invention" did. (As we shall see, that is very significant.)

Writing in *Science* magazine, Leslie Roberts characterized the ability to file such patents as "a land grab, a pre-emptive strike that would promote a worldwide stampede to garner patents on essentially meaningless pieces of DNA." Roberts and others worried that such genetic land grabs would result in scientists hoarding their knowledge in hopes of downstream profits, rather than continuing to cooperate in the worldwide sharing of genetic knowledge that had previously characterized work on the Human Genome Project.

## RELIGIOUS CRITICISMS OF PATENTING LIFE

Religious leaders also criticized allowing DNA sequences to be patented, claiming that *Chakrabarty* failed to understand the symbolism of saying that human DNA could be patented, marketed, and commercialized. The president of the Southern Baptist Convention's Christian Life Commission emphasized that altering or creating new life forms was a "revolt against God's sovereignty and the attempt by humankind to usurp God and be God":

> Human beings are pre-owned. We belong to the sovereign Creator. We are, therefore, not to be killed

> without adequate justification (e.g., in self-defense) nor are we, or our body parts, to be . . . sold in the marketplace. . . . Admittedly, a single human gene . . . is not a human being; but a human gene . . . is undeniably human and warrants different treatment than all non-human genes. . . . Furthermore, the right to own one part of a human being is [all other things being equal] the right to own all the parts of a human being. This right must not be transferred from the Creator to the creature.

As sociologists Dorothy Nelkin and M. Susan Lindee argued, many in religion have come to see human DNA and genes as representing "the social and cultural functions of the soul." They put it this way:

> The gene has become a way to talk about the boundaries of personhood, the nature of immortality, and the sacred meaning of life in ways that parallel theological narratives. Just as the Christian soul has provided the archetypal concept through which to understand the persona and the continuity of self, so DNA appears in popular culture as a soul-like entity, a holy and immortal relic, a forbidden territory.

Notably, this is the same logic that underlies religious resistance to cloning. If DNA is akin to a soul, then copying a genotype of another is inherently evil because it captures the essence of the original and, in making a copy, perverts it.

Of course, these ideas underlie Tomas and the (pre-Henrik) Proletheans' opposition to cloned humans, and explain why Tomas manipulated Helena into killing the other Ledas: As clones, they were corrupt creations of man, perversions that had to be destroyed. In some sense, too, perhaps he believed they had "stolen" the essence of another living person.

## WHY WE HAVE PATENTS, AND WHAT RIGHTS THEY CONFER

To understand what is at stake for the public in patenting DNA tags, it is important to take a moment to consider why we have patent laws in the first place. The two chief reasons for having patents are, first, to reward scientists for discovering new inventions and, second, to promote the general good. The way such inventors are rewarded is by hope of economic gain. Those rewards in turn would encourage other scientists to discover other new inventions that benefit humans.

So strong was the belief that these were good reasons that the founders of American government put them into the US Constitution. Article I, section 8, clause 8 gives Congress the authority "to promote the Progress of Science and useful Arts" by issuing copyrights and patents.

However, it is a common misunderstanding to think that patents confer ownership of the thing patented. No particular thing or class of things belongs to a patentee by virtue of her patent. If Anna owns a bicycle, then that particular bicycle belongs to Anna, but if Mark has a patent on Schwinn unicycles, it is entirely possible that Mark does not own or possess a Schwinn unicycle.

So the DNA tag based on ASCII-coded base pairs that makes Alison or Cosima uniquely identifiable may be patentable, *but Alison or Cosima herself is not owned under patent law.* What is owned is either (a) the right to create a copy of Alison or Cosima, (b) the process that creates such a copy, or (c) both. More important to *Orphan Black,* what is owned is the right to the process that makes not just another Sarah or Helena, but another Kira (and whatever valuable information studying her may yield, such as how to replicate her healing stem cells).

Thus, patent rights do not give complete ownership rights, only partial ones. It is also true that just because I have a patent right does not mean I have the other rights commonly associated with a piece of property or idea. Granting someone a patent on a particular human gene or a DNA segment, for example, does not give the holder of the patent ownership of that gene or DNA segment in all (or any) humans. The holder of the patent would not have the right to extract this DNA from anyone who had it.

Finally, an important function of patents is to facilitate the spread of new knowledge. Once a patent application is accepted, its information by law becomes public knowledge. Anyone can go to the US Patent Office and inspect something's patent to see how it works. Thus, by giving inventors the right to exclude others from making, using, or selling the invention for twenty years (from the date of filing of the application), patents also encourage making the underlying knowledge that led to the invention public.

Thus the Dyad Institute cannot hold patents on DNA tags in the Ledas without making such patents public knowledge—meaning somewhere in some patent office is a public document detailing how and why the Ledas came about, as well as why they claimed creating the Ledas is beneficial to humanity. Otherwise, no patents could have been issued.

## THE USEFULNESS OF A THING PATENTABLE

If originally patents were not supposed to be granted on things that occur naturally in the world, but instead on something created or invented, how then can DNA segments be patented? One answer, from a 1997 survey in a law journal:

> Although patent claims to naturally occurring DNA sequences might be expected to trigger the "products of nature" rule, courts have upheld patent claims covering "purified and isolated" DNA sequences as new compositions of matter resulting from human intervention. Thus, DNA that has been isolated and sequenced in considered patentable subject matter under Patent Statute.

Even so, there is a further test of patent legitimacy: *that the invention has concrete usefulness* and isn't just a theoretical idea. Simple identification or sequencing of DNA segments appears to flatly violate this requirement because knowledge of such segments is valuable only as a research tool, not as a way of making useful products for humans.

This certainly makes us wonder what the creators of the Castors and Ledas truly intended with their cloning project. What exactly was the concrete thing that, to be patented, must have been proven to be useful? Or were the Ledas and Castors patented simply as "research tools"? Based solely on past interpretations of US patent law, that patent would seem almost impossible to obtain (unless somewhere in its application is something about their usefulness that we do not know).

In February 1997, the US Patent Office controversially decided that DNA sequences like the one patented in the Ledas fulfilled the requirement for practical utility because they "were useful for purposes including chromosome mapping, chromosome identification, and tagging genes of known and useful function." This decision was disputed by scientists working for NIH and in academia, who repeated their claim that such DNA segments were useful primarily as tools to further basic research.

Many bioethicists, including this one, thought the Patent Office made a mistake in allowing patents on human DNA tags, first because the patents were on things that really were products of nature, and second because patents had been granted for things with no known practical utility. It would be like finding a symbol for a new car (at least you *think* it's a symbol for a new car) and then filing an application in the US Patent Office for use of that symbol on all cars sold in America, even though you didn't know if any such cars exist or are planned to exist in the future.

In sum, considering the US Constitution, if the goal of granting of patents is to promote "Science and the useful Arts," then such promotion should occur through specific products and inventions, not monopolistic control of *merely possible* future products and inventions. Bioethicists and academic scientists have argued that patenting DNA sequences restricts the free exchange of ideas about genetics. In this particular case, the eagerness of the Patent Office and government to help Big Biotech backfired; it provoked an outcry from bioethicists and scientists working independent of Big Pharm and Big Biotech.

## WHY PATENTS ON DNA FRAGMENTS ARE VALUABLE

Patents on DNA fragments like ESTs are valuable in different ways. Most obviously, the holder of the patent can sell his right to a research company that might use it to develop midstage products like medicine or a diagnostic test for a disease associated with the DNA segment, or to reproduce the DNA segment. For example, the biotech company Amgen obtained a patent for a gene sequence that governed the creation of a protein missing in the blood of people in renal failure (and hence on hemodialysis, a process that cleanses the blood of people with failed kidneys). Through licensing companies to make this protein, Amgen earned $400 million in 1991 alone. And so far, this is mainly how holders of patents on DNA sequences have made money.

Let's take the example of patients who want to test for genes predisposing them to breast cancer. Patients (and their doctors) want complete results; they do not want to be told that a test can tell them they don't have *half* the known genes for breast cancer, but it's too expensive to test for the rest. This means that whoever controls a patent on a particular DNA fragment associated with breast cancer can effectively control all tests by charging a large fee for the DNA fragment's usage. Anyone who wants to develop innovative therapies based on those tests must also pay for use of the patented gene, increasing the money that can be made.

In *Orphan Black*, Helena and Kira obviously possess remarkable powers to heal themselves after injury. Helena is stabbed through her stomach with a steel rod but manages to recover; Kira is hit by a speeding car, taken to the hospital, and soon emerges unscathed. Whatever allows them to do this could possibly be the key to extended life and even immortality, so we are talking about something very valuable—in other words, something big corporations would scramble madly to patent, control, and sell. Because Dyad or Topside owns the patent on creating Helena's DNA—and on creating the half of Kira's that came from Sarah—one of the companies could stand to make quite a bit of money one day in the future . . . especially if any DNA sequence that gives them their healing abilities was human made and not naturally occurring.

## SUPREME COURT MODIFIES *CHAKRABARTY*

In 2013, the US Supreme Court ruled in *Association for Molecular Pathology et al. vs. Myriad Genetics* that human genes for breast cancer were naturally occurring and therefore could not be patented. However, they maintained, new DNA sequences and tags for them *could still be patented*, especially if something new was created that did not previously exist in nature.

Previously, under a patent it was granted for its discovery of two genes that cause breast cancer, Myriad Genetics blocked downstream tests for breast cancer. Any researcher or doctor wanting to test a woman for those genes had to pay substantial fees to Myriad.

So essentially the Court ruled that although *human-made* human DNA sequences are patentable, *naturally occurring* human genes are not, and those who discover such genes (and what they do) cannot patent those genes in a way that blocks others from access to those genes or tests for such genes.

Based on this most recent ruling, could DNA sequences of a Leda be patented in real life? On the one hand, insofar as the Ledas have the same DNA as their ancestor, Kendall Malone, their DNA is naturally occurring and would not seem to be patentable. However, as we have seen, small differences in contributions of mitochondrial genes in the egg that hosts the clone's nucleus and, as we'll discuss in future chapters, differences in gestation and forces that act on the expression of genes, could easily make the DNA of the Ledas different than Kendall's, and moreover, make unique the DNA of *each* Leda. Obviously, because Sarah and Helena can bear children, something about them is different compared to their sestras. Finally, their unique DNA is, in a profound sense, "human made" and not natural, so it might be eligible for patent protection.

On the other hand, a precedent against patenting human beings has already been set. Around 1997, activist Jeremy Rifkin and New York Medical College biology professor Stuart Newman filed for a patent on a human–animal chimera composed of 51 percent animal DNA and 49 percent human DNA. Although they had not created such a chimera, did not know how to do so, and did not intend to do so, none of that is necessary to get a patent. Moreover, the Patent Office was already issuing patents on DNA sequences from animals and humans for which the filers were similarly ignorant.

The application was a *reductio ad absurdum* attempt to test the boundaries of how much human DNA could be patented. Of course, the application created a crisis in the Patent Office. To keep politics out of patents, the Patent Office cannot legally reject a patent on moral grounds. Ultimately, although the Patent Office had previously granted patents on smaller sequences of human DNA, this application was rejected for being "too human"—even though it is not clear that the Patent Office had the legal right to reject the application in this way.

So could the Leda and Castor clones' DNA be patented in the real world? Well, that partly depends on how the various courts in the United States and Canada, including their highest courts, fine-tune their previous decisions. It is predictable that they would allow a patent on a cloned, prized dairy cow, one that produces eighty times the milk of a normal cow. It is much less obvious that a similar patent on producing a superior human being would be possible.

## CHAPTER 9

# "Things Which Have Never Been Done"

## *Eugenics and Clonal Dynasties*

*"We do terrible things for the people we love.
Stop asking why. Start asking who."*
—Beth, "Certain Agony of the Battlefield,"
season three, episode six

$A$ s the philosopher George Santayana famously said, "Those who do not remember the past are condemned to repeat it." To which we might add, "Those who never learned what happened in the past are even more condemned to repeat it."

If you are like most people, you associate state-coerced eugenics—a movement that aimed to improve the population via selective breeding and included compulsory sterilization of "unfit" men and women—with evil physicians under the Nazi regime in Germany. So you might have been surprised when, in season two, *Orphan Black* referenced North American eugenics institutes and their programs by introducing the Cold River Institute and its "Better Baby" photos. But *Orphan Black* is correct in implying that eugenics did not originate in Germany or even in Europe, because, in fact, eugenics started in North America. And just as it was practiced in Nazi Germany to sterilize "unfit" people, so it was used in Canada and the United States.

The North American eugenics movement peaked between 1905 and 1935, but continued much later than people realize; eugenic practices continued until 1972 in North Carolina and Alberta, Canada. (Outside of North America, mandatory sterilization of certain people deemed unfit continued in Sweden, amazingly, until 2011.) Similarly, we learn in *Orphan Black* that the secret projects of Cold River were officially shut down in the 1970s, yet "some continued even after that"—such as Project Leda.

Eugenics relates to cloning humans and *Orphan Black* in a straightforward way. As soon as you start cloning genes, you are immediately forced to make a choice: Who do you use as a source? Rather than letting Nature or God decide which combination of genes becomes a person, some humans now do so. And as soon as that choice is in human hands, we naturally start choosing *against* ancestors with terrible genetic diseases ... and then it is not too far a leap from that to start choosing for other, more subjective reasons, such as choosing the best possible ancestor. As soon as you start talking about "the best possible ancestor" and rejecting certain people as ancestors, you enter the territory of historical eugenics.

So let's go back in history to learn a little about how eugenics began in North America—and then look at how that relates to cloning and *Orphan Black*.

## EUGENICS AND STERILIZATION

In the late 1880s, Charles Darwin's cousin Francis Galton coined the word *eugenics* from the ancient Greek words *eu* (good) and *genos* (birth, origin).

We all remember Darwin for his theory of evolution. One of the best-known elements of that theory is the concept of "survival of the fittest" (the term that scientist and Darwin contemporary Herbert Spencer used to describe natural selection) as meaning survival of the *best adapted*; the word *fit* referred to the adaptation of an organism to its environment, especially in terms of reproduction. An organism's fitness was a measure of the number of offspring it had that survived long enough to reproduce.

From this biological Darwinism, however, arose *social Darwinism*, a very different theory and the basis of eugenics (as well as the source of most of eugenics' ethical and political problems). Social Darwinists mistakenly saw evolution in terms of competition among social groups rather than among individual organisms. Mostly well-off WASPs (like Dr. Leekie and Rachel Duncan), social Darwinists believed that their social advantages stemmed from an innate biological superiority over Africans, Asians, Bulgarians, Greeks, Italians, Irish Catholics, and everyone else. In other words, champions of social Darwinism saw *themselves* as the most fit—which they interpreted to mean that to improve humanity, they alone should be able to breed and bequeath their genes to future humans, and members of other, less fit groups (whether other races or the mentally or physically handicapped) should not. "Survival of the fittest" went from being a description of a process to a prescription for action and a moral imperative. As social Darwinist and prominent New York urologist William Robinson proclaimed in 1910 about the mentally challenged, "It is the acme of stupidity to talk in such cases of individual liberty, of the rights of the individual. . . . They have no right in the first instance to be born, but having been born, they have no right to propagate their kind."

So as you see, the efforts to sterilize the Project Leda clones, and ensure the same for any women who had sex with the Project Castor clones—thus preventing both sets of clones from reproducing—are not so far-fetched as they might seem . . . especially given their origins in the show's Cold River Institute.

In *Orphan Black*, Sarah finds papers about Ethan and Susan Duncan's work in the archives of an old church referring to this fictional institute. But its name is a reference to the location of North America's real eugenics headquarters, at Cold Spring Harbor on Long Island, New York. Charles Davenport, who like Dr. Leekie regarded genetic improvement of humans as a new kind of secular religion, persuaded the Carnegie Institute and, later, Mrs. E. H. Harriman, the widow of a railroad executive and one of the richest women in America, to fund the Station for Experimental Evolution, which maintained a Eugenics Record Office from 1904 to 1939.

From its beginning in 1910, the Station was run by geneticist Harry H. Laughlin, who from his post championed laws to restrict immigration from "inferior" countries and to sterilize "genetic defectives." He had his marching orders from Mrs. Harriman and Davenport, who shared his views.

Eugenics was popular because of a widespread racism during the early 1900s that was so deep and vile as to be almost unbelievable today. The newspaper magnate William Hearst and Theodore Roosevelt thundered against "yellow niggers" who had invaded America from Asia. When Henry Ford ran for president in the 1920s, he promised to rid America of "Jew bankers," whom he accused of causing America to enter World War I and who later, he claimed, caused the Depression.

Most people know that the Nazis sterilized 225,000 "mental defectives," but the American government also sterilized such people. Indiana required sterilization in 1907 of the "retarded and criminally insane," and thirty other states soon followed, led by California and Virginia. By 1941,

36,000 Americans had been sterilized, sometimes for a vague condition called "feeblemindedness" or just for being born into large families on welfare. In 2012, we learned that North Carolina sterilized 7,600 Carolinians between 1929 and 1972. In 2014, North Carolina legislators decided to compensate the seventy-two living victims.

One of the most infamous cases of forced sterilization was that of Carrie Buck. Supposedly mentally challenged like her mother, Carrie Buck had been committed at age seventeen to a state mental institution in Virginia. After being raped by her cousin during a visit home, Carrie gave birth inside the institute to a daughter (who was later determined to be of completely normal intelligence). The State of Virginia then petitioned to have Carrie sterilized because her behavior inside the institution was considered "incorrigible."

Charles Laughlin read one social worker's report that Carrie had a "feeble look" (a catch-all phrase for any sort of mental problem) and concluded, *without ever meeting her*, that Carrie's low intelligence was hereditary. Laughlin then declared that Carrie "lived a life of immorality and prostitution," and that all the Bucks belonged to the "shiftless, ignorant, worthless class of anti-social whites of the South."

Despite a challenge from Carrie's court-appointed guardian, the US Supreme Court in 1927 upheld, in *Buck v. Bell*, the Virginia law permitting Carrie Buck's sterilization. Justice Oliver Wendell Holmes wrote the majority opinion in words that seem shocking today, but demonstrate how ingrained eugenics was in politics and law:

> It is better for all the world, if instead of waiting to execute degenerate offspring for crime, or to let them starve for their imbecility, society can prevent those who are manifestly unfit from continuing their kind. The principle that sustains compulsory vaccination is broad enough to cover cutting the Fallopian tubes ... three generations of imbeciles are enough.

What is amazing, of course, is that this outrageously strong language by Justice Holmes was used to justify invading the body of a rape victim against her will—a woman who was also, by all later accounts, of perfectly normal intelligence—and cutting her Fallopian tubes to permanently sterilize her so she could never have the children she wanted.

Eugenics also motivated the Immigration Restriction Act of 1924, which restricted entry to America of "inferior" peoples from Asia, Africa, Greece, Ireland, Poland, and Italy, and promoted entry by English, Dutch, Scotch, Scandinavians, and Germans. President Calvin Coolidge, who as vice president had said, "America must be kept American. Biological laws show . . . that Nordics deteriorate when mixed with other races," enthusiastically signed this act into law.

While the Statue of Liberty today symbolizes freedom, after 1924 thousands of the world's "huddled masses" had only a glimpse of it before they were sent back to their original countries. And although today we use the phrase "melting pot" positively, in 1924 the phrase scared Americans who were concerned they were being overwhelmed by too many immigrants from strange countries (a phenomenon going on today in France, Greece, Italy, and Scandinavia, which historically have had immigration policies very favorable to people fleeing war and poverty around the Mediterranean Sea or from Africa).

Canada's provinces of Alberta and British Columbia acted much like their American counterparts. The Alberta Sterilization Act of 1928 resulted in the compulsory sterilization of over three thousand "unfit" Canadians between its passing and 2012, when a group of fifty Canadians were the last to be so sterilized. Children of minorities (e.g., children of First Nations peoples) and those institutionalized were the groups most likely to be involuntarily sterilized. Many of these facts about Canada only came to light after a woman named Leilani Muir learned that she had been sterilized in her youth and successfully sued the Canadian government for damages, along the way forcing the country's western provinces to reveal their eugenic past.

After the mid-1930s, eugenics declined in the United States. Geneticist Hermann J. Muller called it "hopelessly perverted," a cult for "advocates for race and class prejudice, defenders of vested interests of church and State, Fascists, Hitlerites, and reactionaries generally."

One of the most renowned American geneticists of the early twentieth century was J. B. S. Haldane—who was also godfather of the modern transhumanist movement, which shares with eugenics a desire to improve the genetic stock of humanity, and is the basis for Neolutionism in *Orphan Black*. Eventually, eugenics became so nonsensical that

Haldane himself spoke out against it as it was being practiced: "Many of the deeds done in America in the name of eugenics are about as much justified by science as were the proceedings of the Inquisition by the Gospels." Advances in population genetics prompted Haldane to famously remark, in criticizing eugenicists of his age, "An ounce of algebra is worth a ton of verbal argument."

## EUGENICS' BAD SCIENCE

What were these false ideas on which proponents of eugenics based their actions?

First, they believed the reductionist assumption that social traits are caused by individual genes—that it is a single gene that causes a woman to be a prostitute, a child to be retarded, a family to be on welfare, or a robber to turn to crime.

Although single genes cause some conditions, such as Huntington's disease, this is rare. Most diseases and traits, if affected by genetics at all, are caused by a multitude of genes acting together (more on this in chapter twelve). And becoming a criminal or a prostitute involves decisions of people, not just biology.

Second, eugenics supporters did not understand *recessive inheritance*. Two people who do not express a trait or disease but each carry a gene for it can have a child who has two copies of the gene and thus does express it. So the sterilization of everyone with, say, cystic fibrosis will not succeed in eliminating the disease, because two carriers who don't manifest the disease could still produce a child with it (in fact, this is typically the case).

Third, eugenics supporters acted from a simplistic concept of evolution, one that assumed it would require only a few generations to wipe out inherited diseases. It took humans millions of years to evolve from the first vertebrates and from the first primates. Evolution paints its pictures on a canvas of billions of reproductive acts occurring over hundreds of millions of years, a picture exponentially more complex than that painted by eugenics (or Neolutionists).

Fourth, eugenicists were ignorant of environmental effects on gene expression. How a gene, or a combination of genes, is expressed depends partly on one's environment: what happens during gestation, in early childhood, and so on. Genes have a fanlike range of expression, called their "norm of reaction." Let's say a particular combination of genes creates a brown squirrel with a yellow streak across his tail. Depending on what the squirrel's mother ate during gestation, that particular combination of genes might produce a squirrel with a large streak or a small one that was a little yellow or bright yellow.

Fifth, eugenics was also ignorant of the role of mutations and chromosomal breakage in disease and developmental disabilities. Eugenicists mistakenly believed that if all mentally challenged people could be prevented from reproducing, their condition could be eliminated from the gene pool. But, due in part to chromosomal breakage, *all* women over thirty-five run a greater risk of having a child born with Down syndrome or other genetic conditions.

Finally, eugenicists did not understand *population genetics*, which is also relevant to debates today about human cloning. Eugenicists hoped to perfect humanity through selective breeding, but population genetics predicts a *regression to the mean*, the inherent tendency in stable populations over time to express the mean (average) value. In vast populations of humans, the "pull" of billions of new births will normalize any deviant values.

Similarly—unless the state were to control who had sex with whom, and thus how and why women get pregnant and bear children—no matter how many seven-foot-tall humans were cloned, after breeding with normal humans for a few generations, their children would be born of normal height.

Population genetics also shows the stupidity of the idea of "self-directed evolution" and enhancement espoused by *Orphan Black*'s Neolutionists. Even if you could modify your genes to, say, become seven feet tall, and even if you could do so in a way that was inheritable by your descendants (a much riskier proposition), those genes almost certainly would not pass into the general population.

## Why Chosen Evolution Through Cloning (Previously) Great People Is Risky

Like eugenics, the desire to clone the genes of great people arises from a desire to produce better, more fit children—to improve humanity. This could easily be a stated goal of the Dyad Institute or Topside. But as the example of cloning great people shows, making genetic choices based on the gene expression of living individuals far from guarantees a child's fitness. So such a goal may be as poorly based in science as the past eugenics movement was.

If we ever can safely recreate the genotype of a great historical person, we will be able to answer an interesting question that was the crux of Scottish philosopher Thomas Carlyle's theory of history. Carlyle argued that history's big events were shaped by great men—men such as Genghis Khan, Napoleon, and Alcibiades, to whom we might also add Adolf Hitler. But are great men great because their genetic nature in and of itself compels them to rise to the top, or are they merely the right DNA (or genotype) molded to the right expression of those genes (or phenotype), appearing at the right time in history in the right place?

In short, would a great man be really great *again*? Would the genotype of Napoleon be a great general, or financier, or just a megalomaniac who ends up in Leavenworth federal prison?

Actually, this question must be separated into two parts: First, would such a man be great, and second, would he be good in the same way, for the same reasons, and for the same people?

These are questions that are not easy to answer, in part because whether a particular man's contribution to a particular society at a particular time and place in history is "good" is relative. Take, again, Napoleon. Was he good or bad for Europe?

As well, recreating the genotype of an ancestor tells us nothing of how that new human would feel and act. Even if we were able to recreate genius—even if the genotype of a Galileo or a Leonardo da Vinci were to again result in a person of extraordinary talents, which is not itself a foregone conclusion—we cannot guarantee that the genius will use those talents for human good. Especially because the new person will have free will, we cannot guarantee any result from recreating his or her genotype.

Because we know genetic essentialism is false, we know that the new person will differ from the ancestor. A person originated from the genes of Gandhi could be very violent; one from those of Mother Theresa, an indulgent narcissist. A rebellious teenage clone might turn against the expectations he received along with his famous genes and form his adult character in such resistance. There are simply no guarantees.

So it would be a gamble to produce a dozen progeny of a modern chemist as brilliant as Robert Boyle. We might get some dedicated to using chemistry to cleaning up the environment or making wonderful drugs to kill cancer, but we might also get others who created synthetic heroin that could be sold for pennies.

## FAMILY-DIRECTED EVOLUTION

But wait! There is another possibility here, one that scares egalitarians and that is far more real. What if Neolutionists could achieve their goal of self-directed evolution not through individuals but through families? What if the families themselves were not duped, but willingly involved? Is that so crazy?

Maybe not. Consider that just by sexual reproduction, NFL quarterback Archie Manning produced two sons who are now also winning NFL quarterbacks, Peyton and Eli. If

Peyton Manning also wanted a great quarterback for a son and was able to clone his genotype, it is easy to believe his clone son would also become a star. (No one would clone the genes of Archie's oldest son, Cooper, whose NFL hopes were dashed by a diagnosis of spinal stenosis.)

Let's consider the example of height again. As regression to the mean tells us, even if you could successfully change your genes and germ cells to become seven feet tall and produce children who were seven feet tall, if your seven-foot-tall descendants married people of normal height, your grandchildren and their children would be normal height. On the other hand, if you originated children by cloning, in a family line over several generations, *you could in fact create a line of descendants who were all seven feet tall*—a cloning-based biological dynasty.

Consider a different example, a hypothetical Adorno family that owns a lot of property in Italy. Each generation has handed down more property to the next, such that today, the family controls billions of dollars. Suppose parents clone the most successful current Adorno real estate investors and then each subsequent generation does the same. In a few generations, the Adorno investors might be so shrewd, so canny, so skilled that they could control all of Italy. Other families might pursue perfection in singing opera, or chess, or physics, but one thing seems certain: If an already successful family chooses to clone its best genotypes and gives its cloned children the best training from an early age, that family will likely be very successful.

Would this be such a bad thing? Well, maybe for society, especially according to those who equate inequality with injustice. John Rawls, the Harvard philosopher and noted egalitarian, wrote in his widely cited *Theory of Justice* that the family contains the greatest sources of injustice, as it will funnel all its resources into advancing the success of its own children while spending virtually nothing on the children of distant strangers.

Many families decide to straighten the teeth of their children with expensive braces. Many spend a great amount of time and money shepherding their children to computer camps, soccer games, and coaching sessions for standardized tests. Can we not extrapolate from these desires to advantage one's own children to further, less superficial enhancements? Is it not inevitable that parents who had the financial resources might seek biological advantages, if available, for their children—ones that could be passed on to their grandchildren as well? For example, suppose Uncle Dewey was fabulously smart, industrious, loved by everyone, and rich. Some families might use Uncle Dewey as an ancestral source for some of their future, cloned children.

When reproductive cloning becomes safe, and when children of the most powerful families in the world—families who know the personal numbers of senators and whose corporations employ professional lobbyists—are infertile, do we really think we can prevent such families from lobbying to create legal ways to reproduce their genes through cloning? Or, if cloning is illegal in North America, from finding another country that allows them to do so? Do we really believe we can prevent scientists everywhere from creating, studying, and manipulating cloned human embryos? Or from studying them with an eye to fixing problems in reproductive cloning? No one can really control who has children, where, and how. And once such cloning is possible, it is easy to imagine some scientist somewhere offering his services to a rich family that wanted superior offspring.

Those at the head of Topside seem exactly to be such rich and powerful families who get what they want. They also subscribe to a transhumanist/Neolutionist ideology that makes them ripe to use cloning and genetic selection to advance their beliefs in the creation of their own children and grandchildren.

Far-fetched? Consider that a middle-class veterinarian in Louisiana made news when he spent $100,000 to clone two copies of his beloved dog. He reports being very satisfied with the result, although the first attempt at a clone died at birth. Should he have spent his money on other things? Well, he had already spent the same amount buying a Humvee, which some people might also criticize, but we generally allow people to spend their own money as they choose.

Of course, cloned human adults would not look or act any different than any other adults and would likely fit unnoticed into families. Early on, in order to protect the secret, astute family might not tell such children of their unique origins and be careful never to have more than twins from one ancestral genotype. Over time, however, descent from a famous ancestor might not only be revealed to the child, but become a source of pride to him or her.

It is hard to ignore the fact that smart, beautiful, healthy people possess many advantages in competing for the prizes of life. And children whose parents *chose* to give them those advantages might feel even more special. Rather than, "Yech, I'm a clone!" it will be, "I'm a clone. You are only normal."

Why might cloning successfully result in such humanity-improving dynasty building, when state-coerced eugenics failed? First, such families already exert enormous control over their children's marriages and childbearing. Some upper-caste Indian families still arrange marriages for their sons and daughters to other upper-caste children with good prospects and good ancestors. Second, some families already heavily invest in their children, especially in the form of education, often making sure they speak several languages and excel in math, science, finance, and communication skills.

## BIOLOGICAL INEQUALITY AND CLONAL DYNASTIES

All of this raises a very important ethical question: Should we try to prevent the wealthy and powerful from using cloning to create biologically superior offspring, lest the result intensify social inequality? Right now, no form of assisted reproduction or cloning can be used to create a Thoroughbred racing horse. Should the same be done to protect our current, rough equality in developed countries? Should democracies fear groups like Topside and its aims?

Where early twentieth-century eugenics was unscientific, public, and coercive, this new option is more science based, private, and voluntary. It is called "stealth eugenics" in bioethics.

If we equate justice with equality, it is certainly true that North America has become a more unjust society over the last decades. In America, *financial inequality* has worsened over this time. There are more poor Americans than ever before, and the income of middle-class Americans has stagnated so much that "*middle* class" seems like a misnomer. Meanwhile, the number of billionaires continues to increase, as do the income and wealth of the top 1 percent of Americans. Add to that the inequality of inheritance, where some children inherit $1 million at birth or, like Donald Trump, get jobs through nepotism that enable them to make $1 million on their first business deal, and you realize that the deck is stacked. Biotech is quite likely to give rich children even more advantages.

It is worth ending here with the huge controversy that rages in the important field of early childhood education as to whether we can do anything at all to help poor children overcome the natural inequalities of genetics—one that engages with an ongoing debate on the impact of nature, or genes, versus nurture, or environment, that we'll discuss further in the next chapter. Head Start, a program run by the federal government to improve the life chances of poor children, is based on the idea that, in terms of life success, genetics are less important than a child's access to things such as nutrition and education. Started in 1965, it bypasses state educational programs, funneling money directly to poor communities for medical and dental care for children, nutritious lunches, and basic social and academic skills. Over the last thirty-eight years, it has tried to improve as many as twenty million American children. But has it been a success?

Alvin F. Poussaint, a black professor of psychiatry at Harvard Medical School who participated in the first years of the program in Jackson, Mississippi, believes that it has. The fact that kids in Head Start were shown to have greater abilities in vocabulary, math, and sociability than kids not in the program proved it was educating poor children and thus would help them escape poverty, according to Poussaint, and therefore it should be expanded. By contrast, Richard Herrnstein and Charles Murray, the white authors of the controversial *The Bell Curve*, think that Head Start should be abolished, arguing that inherited abilities account for all differences in intelligence and success. Murray even argues that Head Start has made minority children *worse off*, by fostering their dependence on government aid.

Similarly, in her book *The Nature Assumption: Why Children Turn Out the Way They Do* (a finalist for the 1999 Pulitzer Prize), psychology researcher Judith Rich Harris argued that Head Start made no difference at all in the lives of children it affected. Why? Because their personalities and intelligence were determined not by their parents or school programs but by their genes and peers.

For those who believe that a just society must promote equality, rather than make it worse, any new *biological* inequality—such as children of star athletes having a greater chance of enhanced abilities through biotech—is regarded as pernicious. It is one thing to tolerate inequities in family support, early childhood education, and quality of K–12 school systems, but deeper, *biological* inequality must be nipped in the bud, especially a metaphysical inequality hitherto unknown among humans: one written not in the shifting sands of unequal environments but in the cold stone of genes. Our society may be able to tolerate *social-economic inequality*, but not tolerate *biological inequality*.

And perhaps this is why Topside must be so secretive about its mission and goals. As Nietzsche said, democracies fear the *Übermensch*, the great-souled person, and would try to bring him down, to enslave him. Democracies would try to prevent such beings from being created. So whether Topside's goal is a cloned superior individual or a cloned superior family line—perhaps the Ledas are just Phase I, where scientists get the kinks out of the process—they must keep their projects hidden from view.

## BEWARE THE *ÜBERMENSCH*?

In short, safe human cloning alarms egalitarians partly because it would allow biological dynasties, which would in turn inevitably worsen existing social-economic inequality. To Cal Morrison, that worsening inequality would mean that Topside won, and that family-directed eugenics had triumphed where state-sanctioned eugenics failed.

To prevent that, egalitarians would make reproductive cloning illegal in all countries. They would join naturalists who fear biotechnology to form a new, powerful coalition against reproductive cloning on the worldwide stage, one that opposes such cloning not because of safety but because of boundary crossings and injustice.

And in truth, egalitarians may be correct to fear a future society in which billions of "normals" propagate naturally, just like their ancestors did for millions of years, the bulk of their children regressing to the mean, while within that society, and increasingly leaving it behind, superior children are advanced each generation, creating a new "genocracy." The jury is out on whether such a situation would be good or bad for humanity, but it would certainly be bad for those left behind.

CHAPTER 10

# Nature, Nurture, and Clonal Identity

I don't know about you, dear reader, but in watching *Orphan Black*, most of the time *I believe that I am watching different actresses*, not the same woman in different hairstyles, clothes, and accents. And even though I knew it was coming, I was still shocked when the bearded, transgender clone Tony appeared at the start of episode eight of season two, a real tour de force of makeup and acting. That one brilliant actress could play so many different roles so well is a testament to Tatiana Maslany's acting, to be sure, but also an illustration of the power of small, theoretically cosmetic changes—a "play within a play," if you will, about nature and nurture. That one woman, with help, could make the same body at the same age seem so different in so many contrasting ways gives us insight into what much larger forces, such as families, countries, and institutions, could accomplish in shaping the same "material."

By having many babies originated by cloning from the same ancestor, gestated by different women, and raised in different places, *Orphan Black* dramatically shows us the difference such changes can make in the way that DNA is expressed. The cloned Leda women are not identical multiples of the same ancestor, but rather "variations under nature."

## NATURE VERSUS NURTURE AND IDENTICAL TWINS

In the last chapter we touched on whether a great historical figure would, if cloned, be great again, and determined that there were no guarantees. Just because a person's genotype—their DNA—is identical to some past individual's does not mean his or her phenotype—the result of DNA's interaction with its environment—will be. But we don't have to clone someone in a lab to prove that. We know for sure this is not true because we have studied nature's clones—identical twins.

Studies of identical twins are the mother lode for determining exactly how much genetics influences adult character. And identical twins who were separated at birth are the most valuable of all in untying the famous nature–nurture knot, because the same genotype is raised under sometimes radically different environments.

Given that the orphans of Project Leda and Project Castor are, effectively, later twins of their ancestor, Kendall Malone, and are one another's genetically identical siblings, what do studies of twins reveal about how such people might be the same, or different, as adults? Which is more important to their development, genes (nature) or upbringing (nurture)?

Whether nature or nurture affects a person's adult character more is a long-standing debate in academia. The battle is ancient and pits giants against each other. Whole institutions and whole fields of study have staked out territory on both sides. On one side, and in fashion today, is genetic essentialism, the "Genes 'R' Us" view that the genes we inherit inevitably shape the people we become. On the other side is the view, whose popularity peaked in the 1970s, that external factors shape us far more than genes—that reinforcement and socialization, family and culture, matter more to who we become than biology.

Politically, a lot hangs in the balance here. Liberals and egalitarians believe, or hope, that biological inequalities (along, of course, with social inequalities) can be mitigated, if not eradicated, by education. Hence programs like the one we discussed last chapter, Head Start, and the establishment of universal, free, public K–12 education. On the other hand, conservatives believe that human nature is set and can only be guided by education, not overturned.

What does the science say?

## WHAT TWIN STUDIES TELL US

Some studies of identical twins separated at birth and later reunited reveal stunning results. The Springer twins were adopted at birth in Ohio by different families and both families were never told, like the orphans of Project Leda, that their child had a living twin. When the two met as thirty-nine-year-old adults, they found that both had been named Jim; married and divorced a woman named Linda, then married a woman named Betty; had a dog named Toy; liked Miller Lite and smoked Salem cigarettes; and weighed 180 pounds and stood six feet tall. Both liked carpentry and mechanical drawing and spending time with their families at the same beach in Florida.

This sort of eerie similarity isn't the norm, however. The most widely known scientific project regarding twins is the Minnesota Twin Family Study, started in 1989, which follows over eight thousand identical twins born in Minnesota between 1936 and 1955 and between 1961 and 1964, plus five hundred eleven-year-old twin pairs, born in 1989, who were added to the study in 2000. (Chances are that it is no accident that sestra Cosima is, when we meet her, a graduate student at the University of Minnesota. Perhaps this university's noted Center for Twin Studies will be used in future seasons of the show.) Most of these twins were raised together, but some were raised apart.

In summarizing the findings of the study in 1990, head researcher Thomas Bouchard looked at the likelihood that two identical twins would be alike as adults, and whether it mattered if they were raised apart or together. Researchers studied similarities in patterns of marriage and divorce, academic ability, personality, substance abuse, leadership, and personal interests. Amazingly, the research showed that twins had a 50 percent chance of being alike as adults, even when raised apart and growing up in different cities with different families. Bouchard concluded that similarities between identical twins were mainly of genetic, not environmental, origin.

## ETHICAL ISSUES IN TWIN STUDIES

Twin studies do have a significant limitation: Like all studies on human beings, they are subject to the limitations imposed by ethical standards of research, especially studies of vulnerable human beings such as children. As such, we can only observe (if allowed to, with consent of their parents) what happens to twins in the haphazard conditions in which they grow up.

To provide the clearest, most scientifically significant results, an ideal (but unethical) study would need to be carefully designed from the beginning so that identical siblings would be separated at birth and each raised apart under controlled conditions, in which none were told the truth. Fortunately, no institutional review board would ever approve such a lifelong experiment, partly because, for many people, being deprived of a twin would seem like a harm.

Nevertheless, if you consider the value of the information twin studies can offer, you can understand why some scientists would be tempted to circumvent the rules. One experiment involving children, which followed many abandoned orphans in Romania after the fall of the dictator Nicolae Ceaușescu, raised profound moral questions because scientists obtained foster parents for some orphans but left most behind as controls. Although this "study in nature" did not itself harm the orphans left behind, critics felt the visiting scientists could have done more for them.

## ARE THE LEDAS AND CASTORS A NEW MINNESOTA TWINS STUDY?

The value identical twins separated at birth offer to scientists would be multiplied many times over by larger groups of identical siblings—like a set of clones. In fact, we could say it would be priceless, a psychological master key that might answer, once and for all, the question of whether genes, or family and culture, contribute more to who we are. A group, say, of eight clones of the same ancestor, gestated by different women and raised in different countries by different families, would provide an incredible base to describe how varying uterine environments, kinds of families (or the absence thereof, in Helena's case), and cultures influence the expression of the underlying genes.

Surely this is one reason that Dyad and Topside employ monitors and keep such a close eye on each of the Ledas. For psychologists studying development, such studies would be immensely fruitful. And for evolutionary biologists and neuroscientists debating the nature–nurture question, such a study might answer some questions once and for all.

No wonder everyone is so interested in the Ledas!

## CHAPTER 11

# Are the Ledas Really Genetically Identical?

*PAUL: There's nine of you.*
*SARAH: No! There's only one of me.*
—"Parts Developed in an Unusual Manner,"
season one, episode seven

Several of the Ledas in *Orphan Black*—Alison, for example, in "Variation Under Nature" (season one, episode three)—say that they are genetically identical. But that claim is not 100 percent true.

How can that be? Isn't having identical genes what being a clone means? In somatic cell nuclear transfer, or cloning, the genes in an egg's nucleus come from a single source that forms the embryo of a future human clone.

We've already discussed one important genetic difference in the Ledas, as indicated by the show itself: the unique DNA tag, added by scientists at the time of cloning, by which each clone can be identified. But there are other ways in which a clone ancestor's genes are not reproduced exactly, or expressed in exactly the same way.

## WHAT CLONING CANNOT REPRODUCE

To begin with, two embryos with the same DNA will always, atomically, reveal minor variations. Atoms combine to form molecules that in turn compose enzymes and proteins. For example, according to most chemists, the probability that any two hemoglobin molecules (the protein in red blood cells) in a human body are the same is close to zero. So even though the greater gene structure of two identical clone embryos would be very similar, at the molecular level there would already be differences.

The probability of any two cloned humans being identical down to their last cell is even lower, because the probability of any two things being exactly identical drops further as those things' complexity increases. When the jump is made even just to the cells that molecules form, much less the bodies composed of those cells, complexity jumps exponentially.

As *New York Times* science writer George Johnson explained:

Even cloned cells, with identical sets of genes, vary somewhat in shape or coloration. The variations are so subtle they can usually be ignored. But when cells are combined to form organisms, the differences become overwhelming. A threshold is crossed and individuality is born. Two genetically identical twins inside a womb will unfold in slightly different ways. The shape of the kidneys or the curve of the skull won't be quite the same.

He does note, though, "The differences are small enough that an organ from one twin can probably be transplanted into the other."

## MORE GENETIC INPUTS

In addition to these differences on the molecular side, there are differences in a cloned embryo's actual genes, depending on the egg into which the nucleus is implanted.

An embryo's genes do not come just from the implanted nucleus. As noted in chapter six, the egg itself contains mitochondria, the energy source of cells, and inside these mitochondria are a small number of genes. Although mitochondrial DNA accounts for less than 1 percent of the resulting person's overall genes, such a contribution so early in life can make a big difference later as an adult. It is like a child growing up with or without fluoride in his or her drinking water; the former can result in almost no cavities for life.

There's also the issue of gene activation. In a female embryo, there are two X chromosomes, one inherited from each parent (or, in the case of a clone, one from each of her ancestor's parents). Early on in female embryonic development, each cell randomly inactivates one of the two X chromosomes: About half of the cells inactivate the maternally derived X and about half, the paternally derived X.

Once a cell inactivates a particular X, that X remains inactivated in all cells descended from it via mitosis. But because the population of cells is not enormous at the time that chromosome inactivation occurs, the resulting distribution of cells inactivating the maternal X and those inactivating the paternal X is not always 50:50. So even in the Ledas, whose X chromosomes are identical, we would see differences in activation. One Leda might express the maternal X in 70 percent of her cells and the paternal X in only 30 percent, while another expressed the maternal X in 60 percent of her cells and the paternal X in 40 percent.

Something similar happens with the other twenty-two chromosome pairs, as well. For each gene on a chromosome, humans have two alleles, or gene variants. Because of something called genetic imprinting, one of those two alleles is sometimes not expressed. For example, a paternal allele can be imprinted and suppressed, so only the maternal allele is expressed. So cloned embryos start to differ from each other very early on.

All these small differences in early embryos caused by genetic imprinting, combined with the presence of different mitochondrial genes from different eggs and, in females, chromosome inactivation, could account for surprisingly significant differences in hair color, complexion, height, and even personality—creating, in the case of the Ledas, many radically different people from Kendall Malone's genes.

Even with cows created from the same cloned embryos, the model that geneticists use to predict similarity in milk production forecasts only a 70 percent match in taste and quantity. And human identity, with many more potential environmental inputs, is much more complex than cow's milk.

## Sarah Manning's Four Mothers

There are four women who might justifiably call Sarah Manning their daughter: Amelia, the *surrogate mother*, the African American woman who gestated her; Mrs. S, Siobhan Sadler, *the raising mother*, the woman who nurtured Sarah from infancy to adulthood (and who, in an act approaching sainthood, totally uprooted her life and moved from Ireland to North America to protect Sarah and Felix from unknown enemies); Kendall Malone, *the major biological mother*, from whose cells Sarah was cloned; and finally, *the minor biological mother*, the woman whose egg was used to host the nucleus of the ancestor's nucleus, whose identity we do not yet know.

Which one of these four women gets to call herself Sarah's "real" mother? Asking the question this way is really just asking which mother is most important, or rather, which element of mothering is most important. From the major and minor biological mothers come the genetic components of who Sarah is; from the surrogate and raising mother, the nurture to the others' nature. All four elements are necessary. Our societal definition of mother assumes one woman will be responsible for all four of these, but that is certainly not the case for many children—not only clones like Sarah and her sestras.

Perhaps the most tactful conclusion is to say that each of the women were *contributing mothers* and *mothers in a special way.*

## THE ROLE OF EPIGENETICS

The most substantial way in which the Ledas differ is explained by *epigenetics.* What is epigenetics? In every human body, there is a layer of proteins called *histones* that wrap DNA; this protein layer is called the *epigenome.* This wrapping carries chemical tags that tells genes when to turn on or off. How tightly or loosely batches of DNA are wrapped in the epigenome shapes the physical structure of the *genome,* activating some genes and shutting down others.*

While the underlying genetic base of all the Ledas is the same, inevitably their individual epigenomes must also vary, because the epigenome is modified by events in one's environment. So, for example, whether certain genes of a six-month-old fetus are turned on, and then expressed,

---

* You can learn more in a wonderful video on the subject by the genetics department of the University of Utah: http://learn.genetics.utah.edu /content/epigenetics/intro/.

depends on things like how the mother eats, her stress level, and whether another fetus inhabits her womb.

Another, maybe better way of putting this is to say that our epigenomes have evolved over millions of years to allow our genomes to respond to the challenges of survival and reproduction in varying surroundings, by expressing the best underlying genes for a specific environment. (A rigid, one-way-only method of gene expression might have doomed humans, who live in sometimes radically changing environments.)

So again, small differences during the formation of the embryo, during gestation, and during the first two crucial years of life, as well as when hormones flood the body during the teenage years, could easily lead to adults who share the same underlying DNA and genes appearing as different as the sestra clones in *Orphan Black*.

For example, the Ledas seem to have different textures of hair. Also, there may be biochemical reasons why the Ledas differ in susceptibility to addiction. We know Alison has such a problem and so does Sarah. But it does not appear that Rachel or Cosima or Krystal do.

Some of the most exciting research in biology today concerns epigenetics and a version of "self-evolution"— though not of the sort promoted by *Orphan Black*'s Neolutionists! This self-evolution concerns what individuals can do to turn on or turn off telomeres, the tips of chromosomes that shorten and thereby age our cells. A ton of research has been done on this topic, and thousands of anti-aging claims have been made, but the distillation of all the research is that two things are good for telomeres in mice and also good for humans: green tea and red grapes (and to a lesser extent, red wine). In other words, drinking green tea and eating red grapes can modify the way your underlying genes are expressed. Perhaps red grapes and green tea activate cancer-suppressing cells or help telomeres stay long. Whatever the mechanism, they seem to have a healthful influence on one's inherited genes (at least, enough of one that I've switched from soda to green tea and from green grapes to red ones).

Almost all other claims about anti-aging schemes fail except one: severe caloric restriction. Such a "survival diet" seems to turn on reserve genes that we've inherited for surviving famine and catastrophe. (We don't know the exact mechanisms here, just that it works with caged monkeys, who, when starved, live much longer.) The obvious problem, however, is that few people want to live on 1,800 calories a day, much less a low-fat, non-dairy, vegan diet of mostly fruits and vegetables. But the impact of the survival diet does illustrate epigenetics: how environmental stresses (including ones we choose voluntarily) can turn on hidden genes and turn off others.

## DELAYED AND CONJOINED TWINS

The late, renowned Harvard biologist Stephen Jay Gould, who is known for his attention to the complex interactions between heredity and environment, once claimed that some living, identical human twins are more identical than cloned humans would be. This is because, for two people to be identical, it would require not only an identical genotype inserted into an enucleated egg, but also the same inheritance of mitochondria in the cytoplasm of that egg, the same womb and exposure to the same unusual events in the womb (e.g., alcohol consumption, falls), and the same parents, in the same geographical place and time. (As Gould asked in a *Natural History* article, "Does anyone believe that a clone of Beethoven would sit down one day to write a Tenth Symphony in the style of his early-nineteenth century forebear?")

Even in cases where the mother is the same, differences in her behavior and environment during gestation make a difference. As I have argued elsewhere, the best way to think about a person originated by cloning is as a delayed twin of an ancestor. Delayed twins are actually something that has happened in reality many times, using assisted reproduction. One of two identical human embryos is gestated to birth by a woman and then, sometimes as long as seven years later, the twin is similarly gestated to birth, giving the firstborn a much younger twin. And as with the Ledas, the environmental differences during pregnancy and beyond always substantially alter the final phenotype of the second twin.

Even in the case of conjoined twins, who originate from the same zygote and share both the same womb and exactly the same environment for life, two people with the same genome sometimes manifest very distinct personalities as adults. Take, for example, the original conjoined twins Eng and Chang, who were born joined by a thick mass at their chests and were never separated. Amazingly, one was a morose alcoholic, and the other, a benign and cheerful man. The two were married to different women and had separate houses in the rural Appalachian mountains of North Carolina. They alternated houses every other week, fathered between them twenty-one children, and lived to the age of sixty-three.

Like Eng and Chang, the famous Tocci twins had different personalities. Like Eng, Giovanni Tocci drank beer in considerable quantities, while Giacomo did not like beer and preferred mineral water. (The Tocci twins had separate livers and circulation; Eng and Chang shared a liver.) Giovanni was introverted and fond of sketching; Giacomo was an extrovert, a big talker, and also had a volatile personality (if he found some fault in Giovanni's sketch, he would kick the drawing off "his" knee). Similarly, the conjoined twins Abigail and Brittany Hensel, who share a common body below the neck, feel hungry and sleepy at different times, sometimes get different grades on exams, and have different personalities, with Abigail describing herself on Facebook as "girly" and "outgoing," whereas Brittany describes herself as "not too girly" and "shy."

If conjoined "identical" twins can have such different personalities, just imagine how different two originations from the same genotype have the potential to become! When identical nuclei are inserted into different eggs, and the resulting embryos are gestated by different women, adopted by different families, and grow up in different cultures or times, the "identical twins" will differ substantially.

## VARIATIONS ON A CLONAL THEME

Was it dramatic considerations or scientific facts that drove the creators of *Orphan Black* to differentiate the various clones as widely as they did? Only they know. But those differences are far from scientifically impossible. While Alison's claim that the clones are genetically identical is somewhat correct, that does not mean that their phenotypes—the embodied expression of those genes—are identical. In resisting genetic reductionism, *Orphan Black* offers a valuable lesson in epigenetics to all of us.

CHAPTER 12

# Sexuality, Gender Identity, and *Orphan Black*

N o one watching *Orphan Black* can fail to notice that the show raises profound questions about the origins of sexuality and gender identity. Why, if the Leda sisters share the same genes, are some heterosexual, at least one gay or bisexual, and still another transgender? What is the show saying? That sexual orientation is a choice and not biological?

Not necessarily. While some fans wonder whether *Orphan Black*'s creators truly thought out the implications of different Leda clones expressing different kinds of sexuality at the start (did they realize how huge this issue is for gay and trans people, or did they just want different, sexy characters for Tatiana Maslany to play?), other astute fans believe that the reason for the discrepancies is that the Ledas are not actually genetically identical and that each contains unique DNA—which would likely be the case in real life, as we discussed in chapter eleven. The clones themselves probably have bigger genetic differences than just the unique DNA tags Cosima discovers in the final episode of the first season, and sexuality may be one of them.

*Orphan Black* is celebrated for its inclusion of LGBT (lesbian, gay, bisexual, and transgender) characters whose story lines do not depend on their sexuality, and interviews with *Orphan Black*'s producers Graeme Manson and John Fawcett and lead actress Tatiana Maslany often include questions about what point the show is trying to make with Cosima's homosexuality. However, both producers and the star of the show usually skirt the issue. They claim that all the clones are bisexual and that nuances in nurture create individual sexual identities.

Some fans find this answer disappointing, claiming the show's creators are avoiding the bigger question here of causes of sexual orientation. And the producers' claims about every sestra being bisexual could be strengthened if, say, in season four or later, we see that Alison had a bisexual relationship in college or Sarah once dated a woman.

As well written a show as *Orphan Black* is, it is hard to imagine the show's writers overlooked the ongoing real-world nature-versus-nurture debate about human sexuality.

In any event, a show featuring so many genetically identical women is one of the greatest devices imaginable to explore how different factors affect sexual orientation and gender identity, and how small differences in gestation or early childhood might profoundly affect them later in life.

## A CAVEAT

I want to confess up front that what scientific evidence there is about the origins of sexuality and gender identity is not only shaky, but contested, probably biased, and constantly in flux.

Especially in America, with its Puritan heritage (versus the more relaxed attitudes of Europe and Asia), it is difficult to discuss these topics without their being politicized. Although this is true of almost any real issue in bioethics, there is something about homosexuality, bisexuality, and being transgender in America that sparks an insane amount of scrutiny and discussion. As such, any account of the genetic or environmental origins of sexual orientation is bound to raise the hackles of some zealots, somewhere.

So with that caveat, we proceed.

## BASIC CONCEPTS IN MODERN SEXOLOGY

Before we discuss sexual and gender identity in *Orphan Black*, it helps to consider some basic concepts and terms in modern sexology. As with many areas of modern life, the terms we use to refer to people's sexuality can create controversy and, as such, constantly change.

Professional sexologists distinguish between gender identity and biological sex. *Gender identity* refers to how one sees oneself: as male, female, in between, or other. *Gender expression* refers to how one presents oneself in public and to prospective sexual partners. Both differ from the idea of *biological sex*, which is determined by one's chromosomes.

Of course, it is possible for one person to have the chromosomes of two different biological sexes. The word *intersex* refers to people with anomalous sex chromosomes, but also people with anomalies of the gonads, reproductive ducts, and/or genitals. This includes congenitally ambiguous genitals, contrasting internal and external sex anatomy, incomplete development of sex anatomy, and disorders of gonadal development. The Ledas and Castors' genetic ancestor, Kendall Malone, for example, is intersex.

*Transgender* differs from *intersex* as internal differs from external. People who are transgender, or trans, feel that their physical body does not correctly correspond to their gender; as teenagers or adults they often (but not always) seek hormones and/or surgery to correct that disconnect. Medically, they feel "dysmorphia" about their bodies. Intersex people, because they have non-normal sex organs, may or may not identify with the gender that corresponds to their external organs. Both groups want the right to define their gender identity and both may seek hormones and surgery to do so.

Why is their right to do this so important? Because our anatomy and gender presentation matter. They limit what we can do (e.g., in sports, what field one competes in) and how we experience the world. Socially, we expect behavior to be based on other people's anatomy and gender presentation. We normalize ourselves each day by the way we cut our hair, dress, and so forth. (An excellent novel about all these issues is the 2002 Pulitzer Prize–winning *Middlesex*, by Jeffrey Eugenides.)

In progressive discussions of gender and sexuality today, an infographic called a Genderbread Person is used to explain ideas about gender and sex and represents what is probably a more accurate picture of the complexities of human sexuality. The figure includes a picture of a heart denoting *sexual orientation*; a picture of a brain denoting *gender identity*; an arrow to the crotch, denoting *biological sex*; and a penumbra around the person, denoting *gender presentation*. For example, an intersex person might orient heterosexually with a female gender identity but possess androgynous sex organs and present as male. A biological male might orient as gay, have female sex organs, and present himself as male. Another biological male might present as female and be attracted only to females.

Finally, *cisgender* is a term used to describe those whose gender identity conforms to their biological sex, whereas *transgender* refers to people for whom it does not.

So thus far, *Orphan Black* gives us one gay clone, one transgender clone, and many heterosexual cisgender clones. Are all these things possible, given an identical genome?

## THREE FRAMES ABOUT THE ORIGINS OF SEXUALITY

Today, three frames dominate discussions of the origins of sexuality and gender identity. The first, the *genetic frame*, says everything is genetic. That frame is exemplified in claims that there is a gene or group of genes that determine whether an adult is gay or lesbian. The second, the *environmental frame*, says that genes don't matter, and it is the early childhood environment—the relationship between parents and child, or early imprinting during key childhood experiences—that determines sexual and gender identity. Finally, the *chosen frame* says that people choose their sexual and gender identity, or if liberated, can choose their identity freely.

## THE SCIENCE OF SEXUAL ORIENTATION

Sigmund Freud famously taught that being gay or lesbian resulted from a child's failure to successfully negotiate childhood and their sexual feelings toward their parents—a clear example of the environmental frame. A male child who overidentified with his mother became gay; a female who overidentified with her father became a masculinized lesbian woman. Today, some researchers, such as Simon LeVay at the Salk Institute for Biological Studies, claim that it is not early childhood but genes that cause a person to be gay or lesbian, just like genes, or a combination of them, cause height, eye color, or hair color—a purely genetic frame. But most scientists agree that, while genetics does play a role, human sexuality is much more complicated than having a so-called gay gene.

In 1957, psychologist Evelyn Hooker completed psychological research widely cited as a landmark study about the biological causes of homosexuality. She gave groups of heterosexual and homosexual patients, matched for age, IQ, and education, three psychological tests (Rorschach, Thematic Apperception, and Make-a-Picture-Story Tests). At the time, homosexuality was classified as a mental illness, so Hooker expected to find a high incidence of mental illness in homosexuals and a normal incidence in heterosexuals, but Hooker found no major differences between the two groups. Her study led to further research on biological versus environmental causes of both mental illness and homosexuality and ultimately to the removal in 1973 of homosexuality from the *Diagnostic and Statistical Manual of Mental Disorders*, aka the "Bible of Mental Illness" for psychiatry, as well as a decrease in the belief that something in the environment was responsible for homosexuality, such as an overbearing mother or a distant father.

J. Michael Bailey and Richard Pillard conducted subsequent studies on sexual identity that documented sexual orientation among identical twins, fraternal twins, and non-twin siblings. They found that identical twins had a 52 percent concordance (i.e., 52 percent had the same sexual identity), non-identical twins of the same sex (who share a womb but come from two different fertilized eggs) had 22 percent concordance, and non-twin siblings of the same sex had 11 percent. This data suggested there is a strong connection between genetics and sexual orientation. However, further research by Bailey found much lower concordance rates for identical twins (20 percent for men and 24 percent for women), suggesting that environmental factors also contribute strongly to sexual orientation.

Studies done by Dick Swaas, director of the Netherlands Institute for Brain Research, found structural differences in brains of homosexuals and heterosexuals: The suprachiasmatic nucleus (a part of the brain involved in controlling the daily cycles of sleep, which may also play a role in sexual activity) was almost twice as large in homosexual men than in heterosexual men. Simon LeVay (mentioned earlier as believing genes to be primarily responsible for sexuality) found something similar. He discovered that a small part of the brain, referred to as INAH-3, was twice as large in heterosexual men as in homosexual men. INAH-3 is a part of the anterior hypothalamus and is known to regulate sexual behavior in male monkeys. But scientists still believe it is unlikely that such differences are themselves the source of homosexuality. Rather, they believe that these differences in size may be a symptom of some other, underlying genetic cause, resulting from the way the brain responds to sex hormones during development.

Dr. Freud isn't the only scientist to have thought sexual orientation is the result only of one's environment. So agreed John Money, a brilliant, iconoclastic psychologist who in the 1960s pioneered the field of sexology at Johns Hopkins Medical School. At the time, behaviorism ruled in psychology and Money strongly believed that a child's early experiences constructed his or her later gender identity. Money taught for fifty-five years at Johns Hopkins, and his work with intersex patients helped its hospital become a worldwide center of sex-change surgery. However, Money faked many of his results, and his advice to parents resulted in great harm to some of his subjects (see *As Nature Made Him: The Boy Who Was Raised as a Girl*).

Unfortunately, real research on how one's environment affects sexual orientation is sparse. Aside from a few biased studies done by conservative groups, the conclusion that environmental factors alone create sexual identity lacks any evidence. The most accepted current theory is that sexuality is more than just genes or just environment, but rather a complex mixture of genetics, biological interactions, and environmental factors.

Cosima Herter, the science consultant for *Orphan Black* and real-life basis for the character of the same name, had this to say about the subject:

> Despite how studies on the genetics of sexuality are represented in the popular press that either decry or redeem the genetic basis of sexual orientation, none of the research to date that espouses to have found the "gay-gene" (or, more recently the "male-loving gene") are actually supported by a claim that one gene, and one gene alone, determines sexual orientation. Sexuality is complex, both as a biological component and a political identity. Our genes do

not define who we are, and while certain genes may indeed be present, they may or may not be expressed depending on a whole spectrum of environmental and biological circumstances.

So here, as is most often the case, the reductionism of either "nature" or "nurture" is too simplistic; neither completely predicts adult sexuality. And in *Orphan Black*, because each clone is subject to different circumstances from conception, many different factors could have contributed to the differences between them.

For example, each sestra (except Sarah and Helena) was gestated in a different womb. In some cases, it appears that exposing a female fetus to testosterone correlates to being both masculinized and attracted to women. According to one study funded by the National Institutes of Health, "The evidence supports a role for prenatal testosterone exposure in the development of sex-typed interests in childhood, as well as in sexual orientation in later life, at least for some individuals." So different exposures to hormones in utero could be a cause for sexual differences between the sestra clones.

Another hypothesis is that human sexuality may depend on cytoplasmic genetic elements present in parts of the female egg, including DNA in mitochondria (as discussed in chapter eleven) and microorganisms present in early cells. In other words, the eggs that Kendall Malone's DNA was put into may have affected the Ledas' later sexual orientations. If the sestras' eggs came from different women, that alone could lead to differing sexual identities.

Finally, there is a claim out there about sexuality that we have not yet discussed, one supported by extremists on both the political far left and far right, that one's sexual identity and orientation are, or can be, chosen or invented, and are created rather than discovered. For some such theorists, nothing is given, nothing is written, and everything is constructed.

But there is overwhelming evidence that this view is false. Rather, the evidence suggests that people arrive in young adulthood and find their sexual attraction set. People do not attend a "sexual orientation bazaar," where merchants offer different sexual orientations to try out. As a thought experiment, the reader need only to consider whether he or she chose his or her sexual orientation, and decide whether he or she thinks people are free to reinvent themselves and be attracted in a way opposite to their present orientation. Indeed, according to the gay philosopher Richard Mohr, most teenagers who are gay, lesbian, or trans find themselves resisting their difference from the dominant cis-heterosexual cultural norm. Their mental health depends on accepting their orientation, owning it, and being proud of it.

## THE COMPLEX ORIGINS OF OUR SEXUALITY

Rather than being a binary, either/or thing, sexual attraction and gender presentation are the end points of a long road of development that has many twists and forks along the way. What led to each of the Ledas taking one fork rather than another may have been many things: different genes added from different eggs and mitochondrial DNA, different exposures in the womb to testosterone and estrogen, different maternal experiences during the nine months of gestation, different interpersonal experiences in early childhood, and so on.

This final spread of development (not unlike the range of genetic expression discussed in chapter nine) is like a fan with a 180-degree arc, where the journey starts from the handle and where, depending on what happened to you before pubescence, you could end up at any point along the outer edge. Along that outer edge are all kinds of sexual identities and presentations, from ultra-femme woman to ultra-macho man to ultra-butch or super-femme lesbian, from strictly heterosexual or homosexual to bisexual, from asexual to omnisexual, and so on. So it is not a scientific or psychological problem that Sarah is aggressively heterosexual, Cosima is a lesbian, and Tony is masculine and transgender. That is simply the reality of who each of us could have been, had our genetic package been tweaked in different ways.

Yes, *Orphan Black* seems to say for its Leda clones, I am of this female body because my genetic ancestor had this female body. Part of me is her body, reincarnated. But I am also different. I am more than her identical, delayed twin. I am different because of small things that happened to me early in my life, before I became conscious of myself as an agent, before I attended school, before my hormones kicked in, and before my first sexual relationship. I may be one of fourteen or more clones, but—much as Sarah insists to Paul in season one, episode seven—there is still only one of me. I, and my sexuality, am unique.

## CHAPTER 13

# Kendall Malone, Chimeras, and Sexual Anomalies at Birth

T he revelation at the end of season three that Kendall Malone is the ancestor of both the Ledas and the Castors seems impossible, some kind of fictional gimmick that could not occur in reality. However, sometimes fact is stranger than fiction.

Kendall Malone is a chimera. The word *chimera*, like *Leda* and *Castor*, comes from Greek mythology and refers to a beast that is one-third goat, one-third lioness, and one-third snake. In genetics, it refers to an organism composed of genetically distinct cells—a person, for instance, whose cells or tissues contain the DNA of two different people.

Kendall says to her daughter, Mrs. S, in the next-to-last episode of season three, "I'm special, you see? [I] absorbed a male twin in the womb when I was formed. I got two cell lines [in] me."

It's easy to imagine how twins in the uterus could become a chimera. If one dies there, it can become a ghost twin ("ghost" because no one may realize the twin ever existed). In this "vanishing twin syndrome," which occurs in 20 to 30 percent of pregnancies where the mother is carrying multiples, the dead twin either miscarries or its fetal tissue is absorbed into the surviving twin. (Incidentally, the dead twin is usually chromosomally abnormal, while the surviving twin is usually healthy.)

In rare cases, the whole chromosomes from the dead twin are absorbed into the other. The resulting person, a chimera such as Kendall Malone, carries two distinct sets of DNA—including, in some cases such as Kendall's, both male and female genes.

## ONE REAL-WORLD CHIMERA

The most famous case of a chimera in recent times is Lydia Fairchild, a twenty-six-year-old woman from Washington State who learned in 2002 that she was a chimera through a bizarre set of circumstances involving a paternity test and legal prosecution. Her story is remarkable.

Fairchild had two children by her husband Jamie Townsend, and then the couple separated. Afterward, Fairchild applied for public assistance, which required a paternity test. The test was required to make Townsend pay child support and also to prove to Townsend that Fairchild's child was his. (The whole case had sensationalistic overtones in rural Washington State because Fairchild was white while Townsend was black, and now Fairchild was applying for public assistance for children. In this state as in many others, to get such assistance, the biological father must be ascertained in order to evaluate the possibility of his giving the mother child support.)

The test proved that Townsend was the father . . . but strangely, even though Fairchild had gestated the children from conception, it showed that she was not the mother.

At this point, things legally got very bad for Fairchild. Even though records from hospitals showed she had given birth to the children, prosecutors charged her with welfare fraud: attempting to scam the government using children who were not hers. Possibly, prosecutors argued, the reason those records existed was because she had been a surrogate for someone else's kids. After all, biology is biology, and who can dispute that? Prosecutors implied she might be trying to claim her sister's or brother's children as her own to get extra money from the state, since the DNA testing showed some genetic similarity, just not enough for Fairchild to be their mother.

The obstetrician who delivered each of the children assured Fairchild that her kids came out of her womb; he was there and would testify to that in court.

While prosecutors pressed to take her children away from her, she became pregnant again. Prosecutors required witnesses to document her birth of a third child, which they did. But like her former two children, this child did not test as her own. Prosecutors suspected some kind of secret switch at birth.

The breakthrough occurred when a lawyer and moral person on the prosecutor's side (not Fairchild's lawyer) discovered an article in the *New England Journal of Medicine* about a female-in-appearance chimeric Boston woman named Karen Keegan. Keegan had needed a kidney transplant and her adult children had volunteered to be tested as possible matches, but after DNA and blood testing, Keegan learned that her children were not her children, which she knew to be impossible.

The Boston physicians tested Keegan's hair, skin, and blood, but none matched her children. Finally, Keegan suggested testing a biopsy of her thyroid, which had been saved in a Boston lab. That tissue's DNA matched her son's exactly.

In other words, the tissue was her son's "twin"—or as some misleadingly put it, Karen Keegan was her own twin. Her adult tissue matched the tissue of the remains of the ghost twin inside her.

So Fairchild's lawyer started getting additional tests. Swabs from Fairchild's parents showed that they were the children's grandparents. And while Fairchild's hair and skin did not show that she was her children's mother, a biopsy of her cervix that fortunately had been kept *was* a match, and the case was dismissed.

# SEXUAL ANOMALIES AND THE ETHICS OF CORRECTION

In the last chapter, we introduced the medical term *intersex*, referring to those born with anomalies of sex chromosomes, reproductive equipment, and/or genitals. Kendall Malone, because she carries a Y chromosome in at least some of her cells, is technically intersex. This is regardless of whether having that Y chromosome resulted in any apparent physical anomalies—which we assume it did not, as Kendall herself did not realize she was a chimera until Ethan Duncan discovered it.

Throughout history, as many as 1 percent of children have been born with ambiguous genitalia, partially formed sex organs, micro-organs, or organs of both sexes (historically called *hermaphrodites*, from combining the names of the Greek gods Hermes and Aphrodite).

For most parents, the arrival of a child that is not clearly a male or a female constitutes a social emergency; even if the parents are comfortable having a child that does not fit cultural norms, they may be concerned for their child's safety, as intersex children are often bullied or battered by their peers. Thus, if such parents are offered a surgical correction at birth, most accept it. Often the child is never told about such surgery. In some cases, this approach works well; with the anomaly "corrected," or given a better appearance, the child lives a happy, unconcerned life. But in others, it causes problems later on, as in cases where the child's gender identity does not match up to the sex chosen for him or her at birth.

The most common cause of intersex is congenital adrenal hyperplasia (CAH), an autosomal, recessive, gene-based disease affecting the adrenal glands. CAH babies lack an adrenal enzyme called 21-hydroxylase, and therefore don't produce enough cortisol and aldosterone, while overproducing androgens. Due to this excess of androgens during fetal development, female children with CAH tend to have ambiguous genitalia.

Without enough aldosterone, which regulates salt retention, all children with CAH experience vomiting due to "salt wasting." This results in severe dehydration and, if untreated, death. Newborn screening in many states picks up this condition, allowing for its symptoms to be mitigated at birth by adding or subtracting hormones or by giving salt. Ambiguous genitalia are often corrected surgically at birth.

Without proper treatment, girls with CAH may be incontinent or have lifelong urinary problems. Treatment includes medications such as hydrocortisone or fludrocortisones to boost levels of hormones. In some cases, female fetuses have been treated in utero.

In bioethics, controversy flared in 2010 when physician Maria New developed prenatal dexamethasone (aka "fetal dex") for use on CAH fetuses. Dexamethasone prevents androgens from reaching the fetus, and hence prevents development of ambiguous genitalia. Research also suggests that women with CAH treated with dexamethasone "show more typical gender behavior" as adults than untreated fetuses. Without intervention, CAH females tend to be tomboyish and more sexually oriented toward other females.

(This further demonstrates how, as discussed last chapter, small differences in environment very early on can profoundly affect later sexual orientation of adults and shows the absurdity of saying adults can choose their sexual orientation. By the time puberty sets in, the orientation of these CAH women—one way or the other—largely has been set.)

Both treatment of CAH and the fetal dex protocol raised many ethical issues. First, was giving female fetuses dexamethasone an unjustified experiment on vulnerable subjects? Second, and more philosophically, what's wrong with being a tomboyish female attracted to women—what is normal and who defines it? Third, should adolescents be kept in the dark about their condition or should they know from the start?

## OVERCOMING SOCIETAL INTERSEX PREJUDICE

As we've seen, many more babies, and hence, many more people, experience variations in genitalia than the public has previously recognized (even if this has been widely known inside medicine). If even 1 percent of babies have some genital or genetic anomaly, then, considering that seven billion humans now inhabit the planet, that's seventy million people, more than the combined populations of Canada and Australia. So there may be more Kendall Malones around than we think.

Yet there is frequently a lot of shame surrounding genital anomalies; hence the secrecy around corrective surgery at birth. Like the adult Ledas discovering—somewhat traumatically—their clonal origins, it can be liberating to have such secrets revealed. For intersex adults who enter puberty feeling dysmorphia about their bodies, learning that they were born a different sex and surgically assigned their present one may make their strange feelings make sense.

If there is one thing the recent interest in transgender people coming out and transitioning indicates, it is that half of the problems of people with gender and sexual differences stem from societal attitudes. Many chimeras such as Kendall, and most intersex people, feel different from and misunderstood by others—and here, too, there is a parallel to be drawn to people originated by cloning. The Ledas' problems, aside from their medical issues, stem primarily from the prejudiced way in which they are treated, especially by Dyad: as freaks, as possessions, as lab rats, and as subhuman.

Someday, perhaps, we will all see people just as people, regardless of how they are born. Let us hope.

## CHAPTER 14

# Would Knowing You Were a Clone Damage Your Sense of Identity?

*COSIMA: You know your clones, we call each other sister.*
*KENDALL: Call yourselves what you want.*
*You're just a bad copy of me.*
*COSIMA: We're kind of over the whole bad copy thing.*
*It's way more accurate for us to call you older sister.*
—"History Yet to Be Written," season three, episode ten

W hat if you suddenly learned that you came about in a way that no human before ever had? What if you learned that you did not really descend from the genes of the woman and man you thought were your biological parents but from a single ancestor, one of whose cell nuclei was implanted in a human egg?

Like the Leda sisters and Castor brothers in *Orphan Black*, you certainly would want answers to a lot of questions. To start, you would want to know *from whom* you were cloned, and why her and not someone else. Next, you would want to know as much as possible about her. Is she alive? If not, what was her life like? How long did she live? What did she die of? Did she have any afflictions that you might have, too? What was her personality, her weaknesses, her strengths? Was she a villain or a heroine to other people?

If she were alive, you would probably want to meet her. Most children want to know where they came from, and any cloned child would want the same, especially since there would only be *one* "parent."

Next, like the Ledas and Castors, you would likely want to know *why you were cloned*. Who hatched this plan? Were their motives good, bad, or mixed? Did they anticipate that you might turn out abnormal? Did they implant more than one identical cloned embryo? If so, what was their reasoning for that? Why not just one—you?

Would it be good or bad to learn that you were cloned? Would you feel it was good or bad to *be* a clone?

Philosophers like to make distinctions. As with scientists, they also like to say, "It depends." Whether you view your identity as a clone as good or bad likely "depends" on *why* you were created—whether you were, as Alison said, "someone's experiment," or whether your creators had higher motives. Viewing your identity as a clone as bad relies on three (faulty) assumptions, which we'll dissect one by one.

## ASSUMPTION #1: ASEXUAL HUMAN CREATION INHERENTLY DEGRADES HUMANS ORIGINATED THIS WAY

Bioconservatives such as Leon Kass and traditional Catholic theologians claim that the reasons don't matter; *any* creation of people through any method other than sex is wrong. Whether it's in vitro fertilization, using harvested donor eggs to create embryos, or cloning, these naturalists think that all such techniques of creating humans are unnatural and forbidden.

Many others long ago jettisoned such views. Why? Because one in eleven couples is infertile by normal sexual reproduction, and if they want a baby that is genetically related to them, assisted reproduction is their only option. To date, more than a million babies have been created with such assistance. Genetically, joining sperm and egg outside the womb in a petri dish, then inserting the new embryo in a woman's womb, is still technically sexual reproduction; the embryo thus created includes two sets of gametes, mixed. But it certainly differs from ordinary sex.

Let's consider, however, another way in which assisted reproduction differs from traditional reproduction: The children created by assisted reproduction know that they were wanted. Barring creation specifically for experimental purposes, a cloned child would know the same.

When children result from parents having scx, the children don't necessarily know that they were wanted. Sometimes (maybe more often than we would like to think) women get unintentionally pregnant and decide to carry the pregnancy to term. I was born in 1948, long before contraception became freely available and abortion was legalized in the United States. So although my mother assured me that I was, indeed, wanted, all I know for sure is that my parents had sex, my mother then got pregnant, and I was born.

In contrast, children created by assisted reproduction or by cloning can *definitely* assume they were wanted. Indeed, people who use assisted reproduction pay a lot of money (usually their own, because assisted reproduction is often not covered by insurance) for this service. Only about a third of couples using assisted reproduction actually end up with a baby, so often the process must be repeated at further cost. So, philosophically, assisted reproduction and reproduction by cloning would be *chosen* conception, not *random* conception, resulting in *wanted* children, not *unwanted* children.

## ASSUMPTION #2: MOTIVES FOR WANTING CLONED CHILDREN MUST BE BAD

In *Orphan Black*'s third-season finale, we learned that Siobhan Sadler's mother, Kendall Malone, is a chimera and the original ancestor of both the Ledas and the Castors. But *why* was she chosen? Does the reason she was chosen indicate anything about the original purpose behind Projects Leda and Castor? What special qualities did she have?

Hopefully we'll get some answers to these questions in season four, because what we do know about the motives for creating the Ledas and Castors is minimal. Because the Ledas' unique DNA is patented, we assume Topside and Dyad are interested in using them (and their unintended progeny) to make money in some way. We also know Ethan Duncan seems to have regrets about his role in the process, given that he sacrifices his life to prevent Topside from getting its hands on what he knows. As the end of season three revealed that Susan Duncan still lives, perhaps season four will reveal her motives. But the evidence suggests that the motives behind creating the Ledas are not good.

*Orphan Black* has also imputed negative motives to the creators of the Castors, whose aim, based on the Castors' military training and on the conversation between Paul and Dr. Coady about their infectious protein, appears to have been to create living weapons that can be directed at enemies.

The literary associations of bad motives with creating cloned children so often overwhelm us that we sometimes find it hard to imagine good motives for anyone wanting to create a child by cloning. However, if we take a wider philosophical perspective, outside of *Orphan Black* and other stories, it is easier to see that not every would-be parent of a cloned child necessarily has bad motives. If we view cloning itself neutrally, as just another way to create children, we understand that parents could easily have good motives in creating children by cloning, such as avoiding genetic diseases in their families or hoping to recreate traits of a revered ancestor.

## ASSUMPTION #3: GREAT EXPECTATIONS AND CLOSED FUTURES

This leads us to another question hotly debated among people who write about cloned babies: Would a child created by cloning have certain expectations placed on her—specifically, would she be expected to be like her ancestor? And would such expectations be bad for that child?

There is a common objection to cloning that I call the *objection about a closed future*. It says that all cloned children would be harmed by the expectations of their originators. A child originated from the genes of LeBron James would be expected by his parents, physicians, relatives, and friends to grow into a star athlete, not a rabbi. A child created from the genes of Taylor Swift would be expected to be both beautiful and talented in music.

A massive number of critics claim that because the ancestor of a cloned child has lived before, and because the child was presumably created because of the ancestor's particular characteristics, the child's future will be closed in a way that has not been true for every other human child who has been born before.

This closed-future objection assumes that a child should be wanted in and of herself, not for the particular characteristics she might have. Every child, critics of cloning say, should have a completely open, completely indeterminate future, a future not shaped by her creator's expectations.

But, again, facing parental expectations is not an issue specific to cloned children. Let's take a more prosaic example: Say, for example, you got a perfect score on the SAT and everyone expected you then to go to college and do brilliantly. What if you decided not to attend college? Or what if you didn't do so well there?

This objection also seems to assume a historical situation in which would-be parents lack all choice or control over their future children's traits. But today we can choose between a healthy baby and one with a lethal genetic disease; given that, is it wrong to choose the healthy one? If not, what is the underlying justification for letting nature's randomness have its way?

Suppose prospective parents have good evidence that a child grown from an embryo containing the genome of Hillary Clinton will likely be intelligent and a child grown from one with the genome of George Clooney will likely be beautiful. Is it evil to choose those embryos for these reasons?

Critics argue that selecting characteristics of children is wrong in one of two ways: either intrinsically, or because such choices will create undesirable consequences for the child.

People who believe that choosing characteristics is intrinsically wrong often believe that it is up to God, nature, or evolution to determine who is born and with what characteristics, and it is wrong for humans to make such choices. But these people often confuse the claim that *society* should not make choices about which characteristics are desirable in human beings with the claim that *particular parents* should not make choices about a child's characteristics. These claims differ a lot. The first takes away reproductive choice from couples and is eugenics. In contrast, the second *expands* reproductive choice for couples. Fears and concerns about the first do not justify curtailing the second.

Moreover, most people don't believe it's wrong to choose the characteristics of future children. In how they marry and plan to raise children, future parents make choices about which traits are desirable, and then later, when trying to conceive and after birth, try to bring about such characteristics. Prospective parents use genetic tests on embryos and fetuses to detect severe genetic disease and often abort those testing positive. During pregnancy, to help their fetuses be born normal and healthy, mothers avoid cigarettes and alcohol. Once children arrive, their parents—based on beliefs about desirable characteristics—send them to one kind of school rather than another, for example a religiously oriented school versus a magnet school emphasizing the arts.

Arguing that such choices are wrong also means accepting *reproductive fatalism*, the idea that one must accept any pregnancy that comes along and, with that, the characteristics of any child that results. Women who get unintentionally pregnant have endured reproductive fatalism for thousands of years. (Unsurprisingly, those who oppose genetic choice also oppose abortion and contraception. At least here, they are consistent.)

The second reason that people argue against choosing characteristics of future children is that they believe such choices will create undesirable consequences for the child. They object that some parents might put too much weight on one characteristic, such as intelligence or their ideal of female beauty, and then be very disappointed when the child does not measure up. They fear any child who lacks the desired characteristics will be rejected by the parents as damaged goods.

Ultimately this objection boils down to the claim that because some parents will conceive children based on ignorance, prejudice, or false expectations, we should block a whole new way of conceiving children. But if these suffice as good reasons for preventing people from conceiving, *then almost all conceptions should be blocked.* Most people on the planet do not think a lot about whether and how they should have children. Whether to saints or sinners, sober parents or drunken ones, children just (amazingly!) come.

## GROWING UP CLONED

Almost all criticisms of human cloning assume that discovering that you are a clone would be traumatic. But can we imagine the opposite, that such knowledge might be a *good* thing?

*Orphan Black*'s characters express mixed feelings about their clonehood. As discussed, in the third episode of season one, "Variation Under Nature," Alison screams to Sarah, "We're clones! We're someone's experiment and they're killing us off!" suggesting self-loathing. On the other hand, most of the Ledas—and certainly Sarah, Cosima, Alison, and Helena—benefit from the companionship of their sestrahood.

Critics of human cloning consider multiple copies of an ancestor being born and raised at the same time as a worst-case scenario, because it is supposedly damaging to suddenly discover there are two, three, or four copies of "you" walking around, as happens in *Orphan Black*. But as we know from the science and see in the show, these copies would be far from identical. If each clone had a different surrogate mother, then each would have different mitochondrial genes, epigenetic programming, and uterine influences. Each would presumably be raised in a different family—each with its own interpersonal dynamics—and some might grow up in different cultures. So even forty embryos gestated from ancestor Chris Rock might be very different when some chanced to meet at age twenty.

And even if some of these embryos were raised together, would that be such a bad thing? Suppose five grow up together. We know that twins develop a strong sense of intimacy, one more intense than other sibling pairs. So a set of five identical children would very likely have strong bonds and close relationships. What a support system they would have! Hard to believe any of them would ever experience the loneliness of an only child.

Over time, some individuals of a group of clones might choose to perpetuate the ancestral line. (Of course, if cloning were available, this choice would be solely up to each individual; it would not be a group decision.) This would be especially true for female clones, who could easily carry on a mother line, creating a kind of family dynasty. Instead of pejorative names like "alphas" and "betas" for assembly-line babies, we can imagine that members of such dynasties might proudly identify as Gershwins (from composer George Gerswhin) or Hamms (from soccer star Mia Hamm), such that over time, these familial names conveyed the emotional richness of today's "Spielberg," "Angelou," "Einstein," and "Roosevelt."

So being a female in a cloned line of female Rockefellers that went back centuries might not be a bad thing. Indeed, the opposite seems likely; if this line prospered and their genes passed on, the descendants would probably enjoy riches, fame, and good health.

## THE PRIME IMPORTANCE OF MOTIVES

One way of summarizing the above discussion is to say that, when it comes to a child's feelings about herself, *how* she was created does not matter as much as *why* she was created. In other words, *motives* are what matter. Good motives are good for creating children and good for them as they grow, whether the children were created sexually, by assisted reproduction, or by cloning. Bad motives are bad for creating children and bad for raising them.

Moreover, if the alternative were nonexistence, few children would complain about the novel circumstances of their birth. From the point of view of harm and results, any life with a little happiness trumps no life at all.

In contrast, a child might rightfully complain if her parents had bad motives in creating her, *regardless of the way she was originated*. Suppose a parent told an adult child, "I didn't really want a child, but I did want someone to take care of me in my old age," or said, "I mainly had you so something of me would continue after my death." These are bad reasons to have a child (cloned or otherwise), and bad things to say to your adult child; such an adult child might justifiably resent being conceived for such reasons. So, too, the Ledas justifiably resent Dyad and Topside and their apparently sinister motives.

The model here should be that of enlightened parents such as those of Brittany and Abigail Hensel, stars of the TLC reality show *Abby and Brittany*, who were born in 1990 conjoined as dicephalic parapagus twins: joined at the hip, sharing some organs, but each having a separate head and operating one leg and one arm apiece. From the start, their parents taught them that stares, jokes, and prejudice against them were society's problems, not theirs. The healthy attitude of the parents has helped these kids develop healthy, functional attitudes toward the unique circumstances of their life.

Surprisingly, when you read most of the ethics literature about human cloning, almost all the objections do not concern *physical safety or physical harm* to cloned children, but instead concern the *psychological harm* of having the identity of a clone. Almost all such objections assume bad motives by those who want cloned children, or assume a society that regards cloned children as beings who either have been mentally traumatized or who will be considered objects of scorn by most people. As we've seen before, this kind of objection begs the question by citing prejudice as a reason for forbidding something. It's like saying, "People will regard children with disabilities in negative ways, so we shouldn't allow such children to be born."

So whether a person originated by cloning would have a damaged identity because she is a clone is not a closed question but an open one, not a given fact but a dubious assumption, and not a foundation for laws but something instead to be overcome in the long march to regarding all humans—regardless of how they were created—as equal moral beings.

As many of the Ledas demonstrate, even with evidence of being created for bad motives, it is still more than possible to live a rich and (we hope, in the end) happy life.

## CHAPTER 15

# Kant's Personhood and the Formation of a Clone's Identity

*VIC: Alison, she thinks there's five of you!*
*DONNIE: There's eleven-ish.*
—"Things Which Have Never Yet Been Done,"
season two, episode nine

W hether a child created by cloning were raised (1) as an individual or (2) as part of a group of other cloned children with the same parent(s) would make a great deal of difference to her future personal identity.

We know this because psychologists have extensively studied twins, especially those twins who were raised together and experienced problems leaving their childhood "twindom" to form individual identities as singletons. Knowing you are one of multiple genetically identical people affects your core identity. What is true for twins raised together would be even more true for larger numbers of identical children raised together, like the Castors. And what is true for adult twins trying to live as individuals might also impact the Ledas.

But first, let's consider a very important point about personhood, as defined by the philosopher of the Enlightenment, Immanuel Kant. For Kant, the philosophical heart of authentic personhood is that it is *chosen* and not imposed—that people should make choices about who they are rather than having it imposed on them by external forces or other people. This idea is central to Kantian ethics and grounds his ideas of autonomy, free will, and rationality.

As we shall see, for an identical twin raised together with her twin today, it may not be so easy to become authentically a person in Kant's sense. We can infer, then, that for a Leda or a Castor to gain such authentic, Kantian personhood may not be an easy task.

## THE SHARED LIVES OF TWINS

Delving into the special nature of twins gives us many insights into how cloned children raised together might feel about each other.

First, there is what psychologist and therapist Joan Friedman calls the "twin mystique." Friedman, a twin herself and mother of twins, specializes in helping twins confront twin-specific problems, especially establishing their own identities as singletons.

The twin mystique as encountered in literature is the idea that twins possess a special telepathy that allows them to read each other's minds and finish each other's sentences and that they share a magical, insuperable bond. But even in the real world, twins are presumed to be each other's best companions, in childhood and beyond, such that they need neither the friends nor socialization of singleton children. In extreme cases, they are made to dress alike, wear their hair the same way, and always go out as a pair, preventing them from establishing individual identities.

"Together they comprise a singular entity—two as one," Friedman writes, concluding that this twin mystique thwarts our understanding of what twins actually experience and hurts their attempts to develop as individuals.

If you read some of the nonfiction books written about twins from the 1980s and 1990s, it is very clear that some parents thought of their twins in unhealthy ways: They insisted they dress alike and wear their hair alike as late as sixteen years old; they insisted they be placed in the same classes in school and go to the same college and room together; they even hoped they would marry and live side by side in houses on the same street.

"Oh, my gosh!" Friedman quotes one parent looking back on raising her twins after they had become adults. "We just got so much attention when we took the twins to a mall." Some parents of twins even refused to refer to each child by name, preferring either to always call them "the twins" or worse, an amalgam of the names of both, such that one of the first-grade boys described actually thought his name was "KeithandDavid."

The most popular assumption in our culture about twins is what could be called the *soul mate view*: the assumption that your identical twin is meant to be your lifelong best friend and confidant and that the two of you shall never part. People constantly assume that identical twins are always deliriously happy to be (1) twins, (2) identical, and thus (3) with each other constantly.

Unfortunately, the reality is much more complex. Having a doppelgänger can be a benefit, but for some individuals, it can also be a ball and chain around the neck. Because twins are expected to be alike, any little difference of opinion can be magnified and become a source of friction, like a small piece of grit or stone in one's shoe. And if one twin keeps obsessing about the difference and bringing it up to the other, the tiny, original irritation can grow to a major sore. According to Friedman's work with such identical twins, this is most likely to happen where one twin sees any difference of opinion between them as a threat to their joint, shared identity as twins.

You can only imagine how much worse this might be if you had not just one but, say, seven twins, and were raised in a collective, like the Castors. How could it not be detrimental to your later sense of self if your parents and everyone else presumed that, while growing up, you needed no other children to play with and that the seven of you would always agree about everything? And it would be even worse if your other six siblings came to agree with this view.

With existing adult twins, when one twin wants to form friendships or engage in activities alone, or starts dating (especially someone that excludes the other twin), such identity-forming projects may seem alien to and threaten the other twin, creating great tension. When the breakaway twin attempts to pursue such projects alone, she may subsequently feel guilty—a traitor to her twin and their special twindom— and forgo the breakaway to preserve twin harmony.

According to Friedman, twins raised together learn at an early age to compromise for the sake of the twindom. Among septuplets, such compromise would be essential. Compromise for their "septdom" must reign or the septdom cannot function. Otherwise, chaos might easily rule and undermine their group identity.

But another word for compromise is control. And if one twin raised alongside another can exert tremendous control on the other, imagine what six could do. You would not really need external authorities like parents or teachers to prevent any one sibling from wandering; the other six would be an incredibly strong leash. Any clone in the septdom attempting to leave and forge a separate identity would be roped back in by any means possible. We see this with the Castors, when Mark tries to leave the Castors for a new life with Gracie, and Seth is sent to retrieve him. (At the end of season three, Mark has resolved the tension between his desire to break free of the other Castors to be with Gracie as a normal heterosexual couple and the pull of the Castors' group identity, not by *leaving* the group, but by reuniting with the group and having Gracie *join* it.)

Many existing twins reared together develop separate roles within their twindom, or twin-entity, especially over decades of life. One may be the Responsible One and always remind the other one of deadlines. One may be the Social One, who is more comfortable with other people and must always get the lagging twin to engage with other people (and who may experience pangs of guilt when her twin is left alone and feels lonely).

Imagine how much more defined such roles might be in identical septuplets. Small differences at birth and arbitrary events growing up would create specialized roles within the group: one as spokeswoman, one as decision maker, one as arbitrator of conflicts, one as the empath, one as the risk taker, one as the athlete, and even one as the contrarian, such that her very identity was in constantly deriding the group for being a collective and not becoming singletons.

We already see different roles developing among the Ledas, even though they weren't raised together: Sarah is becoming the decisive leader of the group, even though she previously always considered herself a loner and not a member of anything. So, too, Cosima has adopted the role of wise "older" sister, almost a caretaker at times, whereas Alison swings between obsessive-compulsive attention to detail, order, and caution and wild, impulsive behavior. Finally, Helena is like the Freudian id of the group, acting from emotion rather than thought, as well as their protector—their (avenging) "angel," as Kira describes her in season one.

Among identical twins raised together, expressing anger at such set roles can be an unforgivable breach of the hidden contract. It may go without saying that many twins have trouble expressing anger, guilt, or resentment about being or having a twin. Rather than honestly admitting such feelings, twins often argue about small things, which then get magnified beyond their real significance.

Even something as simple as saying, "I need to be alone tonight in my own room," can seem, to a dependent twin, cold and hostile, leaving that twin feeling betrayed and angry. As one female twin I know says, "When my twin won't share her life with me, I call her a 'twitch.'" (The portrayal in movies and literature of one twin as the "evil twin," who kills her twin's interfering boyfriend or even, in extreme cases, the other twin, is not therefore without some kernel of truth.)

On the other hand, it is unimaginable to singletons how emotionally close twins feel to each other. It would be as if there had always been another "you" there: in utero, at birth, in kindergarten—forever. No feeling of existential aloneness for you.

Certainly, twins' closeness can become pathological. Consider what one real, male twin said to his therapist about similar subjects: "I never give priority to my girlfriends—never. And even though I can't wait to have a wife and kids and become a dad, I want my brother to be there when I do.

I would still want him as a very close part of my life."We see a magnified reflection of this in *Orphan Black* when Castor clone Miller invites his clone brother Seth to also have sex with a girl that Miller has brought back to their hotel room. And who knows, at this point, how Gracie will be integrated into what's left of the Castors?

In analyzing the mental health of adult twins, Friedman distinguishes between two bad states, *codependency* and *enmeshment*, and the ideal, *authentic closeness*. Codependency, in which the essential jobs of life cannot be accomplished without another's assistance, is bad because it implies that each twin depends on the other to do everything, from trying out for the debate team to graduating from high school. Enmeshment, in which every detail of one's life is entwined with someone else's, is worse—the feeling that each twin cannot exist without the daily presence of the other. Think two sets of five fingers interlocked forever. Think Seven of Nine in *Star Trek: Voyager* and the Borg.

For some twins, the ties of codependency can never be broken. As one twenty-ish twin, who tried to live alone before relenting and returning to living near her twin, was quoted by Friedman as saying, "I'd rather be happy and dependent than independent and unhappy." Again, imagine how uncomfortable it might be, after living all one's life with six sisters or brothers, to live alone and cut off from them. Most identical twins raised together describe separations from each other—whether going away to separate colleges, parental divorce, or one twin getting married—as causing major anguish.

An enmeshed twin who is unable to conceive of life without her identical mate can feel compelled to disclose every intimate detail of her personal life to her twin. Sometimes the purpose is confessional, where the confessing twin seeks to hear from the other, "Oh, that's really not so bad. I've done that, too." At other times, it may feel unbearable to hide anything, no matter how trivial, from the other twin, as if doing so was the first step down the slippery slope of becoming a singleton.

Finally, there's the ideal state, authentic closeness, which allows each twin to pursue an independent life as a spouse, parent, and career person without feeling guilty about not being around the other twin and while maintaining a strong connection. Authentic closeness allows one twin to move to the other side of the country without making the other twin miserable or feeling miserable herself.

However, this state of authentic closeness can be very hard to attain. Friedman relates the story of two female twins in their thirties who attended the famous annual Twin Festival in Twinsburg, Ohio. There, they witnessed twin sisters in their sixties and seventies who had no other close human friend, husband, or acquaintance other than their twin. Shocked at this picture, which they found awful, they immediately decided to work on separation. But when they tried to do so, their parents surprisingly resisted the idea—showing that parental expectations can be as powerful as expectations among the twins themselves. When they did succeed in separating enough that one twin married and had a child, problems still persisted, as when the new mother always assumed that her twin would babysit her child and always be around it—a task the other twin resented.

Even in twin relationships that involve healthy separation, deviant behavior in one twin can profoundly affect the other, healthy twin. Consider, for example, if Beth had been raised with six other Ledas. Her suicide might be perceived as an unforgivably selfish act, as one twin often does when the other kills herself. And as with all such suicides, survivors feel guilty, as if they could have done more to prevent the death. Even without having been raised with Beth, Sarah and Cosima still feel guilty about her suicide.

Similarly, if Alison were to start using the drugs she sells and become drug-dependent, or return to drinking and develop full-blown alcoholism, it would likely be difficult for the sisters to deal with. Often, mental illness is not recognized for what it is and might be perceived as an unjustified decision on Alison's part to pull away. And if Alison were to be hospitalized again, say, for heroin addiction, the other Ledas would no doubt feel obligated to become Alison's caretakers.

How would a similar downfall affect our hypothetical cloned Septdom? Obviously, a great deal would depend on how they were raised. If they were raised communally as a group, as was done in parts of Israel on a kibbutz from its founding until the late 1980s, it would matter a great deal how much the parents were involved, and how effective they were. Parenting seven cloned siblings would be a big task, maybe too big. In such situations, one or two of the siblings might need to assume a parental role. This often happens with normal twins when parents are not around.

## The Importance of Being an Unrepeatable Event

Let's raise one more way that learning you are a clone could impact your identity: It could make you feel less unique. If only one of you was cloned from an ancestor, perhaps this would not be the case; you would be the only clone of that ancestor, and special for that reason. But if many others were also cloned from the same ancestor— if you learned that not only you but *a thousand* other young women were created from the same ancestor—you might experience a dilution of specialness.

It is this lack of uniqueness that the Vatican cites, among other reasons, for condemning human cloning in 2004: "The manner in which a cloned human being has been brought into the world would mark that person [as] a replacement rather than an unique individual . . . a replaceable consumer commodity rather than an unrepeatable event in human history."

Similarly, Rachel feels self-important because she is (or so she has been told) the only *self-aware* Leda clone. It would certainly bring Rachel down a peg or two if she were to learn of thousands of other self-aware Leda clones.

# CHOOSING PERSONHOOD

Many of the moral problems that we have been discussing stem from one huge ethical problem, a problem that needs to be stated plainly and brought out into the open: that there is something major in the relationship between identical individuals, whether two or seven, that is *involuntary and unchosen*. Anything that is imposed is like a shackle.

To be free in the classic sense of autonomy of philosopher Immanuel Kant, obligations, like twindom, must be freely chosen.

Whether it is the assumption that twins will live together, dress alike, be each other's best friend, or care for each other for life, and whether the twins make these assumptions or their parents do, all these assumptions are *imposed* on twins—starting at an early age when they are vulnerable and immature—not chosen.

Only if such relationships are freely chosen as adults can they be ethical. To make two analogies: Noted philosopher Jane English, in her essay "What Do Grown Children Owe Their Parents?" answers, "Nothing." Just because someone created you and raised you does not mean you are obligated to sacrifice your life for them. Why not? Because you were never given a choice in the deal.

Similarly, many Protestants believe that baptism at birth is meaningless and instead should only be done when an individual is old enough to understand what it means and to what he is consenting. In other words, baptism should follow an adult's decision to be "born again" and accept God, rather than having that acceptance be assumed at birth.

Here there is an additional pressure on cloned multiples that would not exist for the naturally occurring variety. Due to being genetic identicals of a preexisting ancestor, it is likely that they would have many additional assumptions imposed on them—a clone of Carli Lloyd, for instance, would contend with expectations of skill at, and love of, soccer. These expectations, too, can only be ethical if, as adults, cloned individuals are allowed to freely choose their relation to them.

So what about the Ledas and their relationships to each other? Given their shared genome, they could have seen each other as competition for who is the "best," or dwelled on who was first, the "original," as Helena did at first. They could have let themselves be brainwashed by Dyad, as Rachel was by Aldous Leekie and Helena was by Tomas and Maggie Chen. But instead, most of them seem to have chosen to see each other as sisters. And if they have indeed chosen that, that would indeed reflect an authentic, Kantian closeness.

# "When Did I Become Us?"

## Group Identity as a Leda or as a Castor

So far we have not discussed one extremely important aspect of being a clone in *Orphan Black*, an aspect that may or may not be true for future individuals originated by cloning but one that could be very important: group identity. The Ledas, upon learning of each other's existence and meeting each other, come to have a group identity. The Castors seem to have been raised with one.

## THE ROBBERS CAVE EXPERIMENT

First, let's take a moment to better understand the formation process of such a group identity.

The Robbers Cave Experiment, the most widely known example of a theory in social psychology called "realistic group conflict theory" (and an experiment that, like the infamous Milgram experiments on obedience to authority or Zimbardo's prisoners-and-guards experiments, probably could not get past institutional review boards today), provides a classic example of how quickly individuals form a group identity. In the early 1950s, researchers took twenty-two white, middle-class boys aged eleven or twelve, who had never met before, and had them live together as two groups of eleven for three weeks in Robbers Cave State Park, Oklahoma, in a two-hundred-acre summer camp.

At first, the group of eleven were just eleven individuals, but once researchers made the two groups aware of each other and started competitions between them, such as tug-of-war and setting up tents quickly for valuable prizes that only one group could win, they became something more than just individuals. At this point, the groups named themselves Eagles and Rattlers, and tensions began between the two. The names they chose became associated with qualities group members were proud to possess: for Eagles, modesty, prayer, and non-cursing; for Rattlers, braggadocio, emphasis on masculinity, and exaltation of combat.

Perhaps the most interesting aspect of this group formation is the importance for bonding of having something to be *against*. So the Ledas bond against Dyad and Topside, and maybe against a world that, if it were aware of their existence, might be against them. Similarly, the Castors seem to have been raised seeing everyone in the world as their enemy except their "Mother" Coady. This "us against the world" mentality and feeling of being under siege by outsiders fuels a close-knit bond.

It also fuels further conflict. In the Robbers Cave Experiment, the two groups soon began raiding each other: They captured, burned, and shredded each other's flags. At one point, just as Philip Zimbardo had to stop his experiments when Stanford students role-playing as guards got carried away and started abusing students assigned to play prisoners, researchers had to intervene to stop one group from attacking the other with rocks.

## CULTURE AND GROUP IDENTITY

The distinguished Ghana-born philosopher Kwame Anthony Appiah uses the Robbers Cave Experiment to describe how social identity arises in groups (see his *The Ethics of Identity*). In particular, he stresses that in the experiment, each group's name, hostility toward the other group, and conflicts with that group *arose in just four days*.

It makes you wonder what could happen over years to a bunch of women bonded together by the same genes, who realize they were created by secret experiments, and who have common, real, dangerous enemies. Makes for a very powerful tribe.

Appiah also uses the Robbers Cave Experiment to make a bold conjecture: that identity precedes culture (I do X because I am Y), not—as commonly supposed—the other way around (I am Y because I do X). The culture of the group is emphasized only after a social identity is formed in response to conflict with another group. So the Malay people of Indonesia and Thailand only came to know each other as such after the arrival of the Chinese—and so Sarah Manning first came to identify as a Leda, as a member of a cloned sisterhood, in response to their shared mistreatment by Dyad and Topside, after which point she and the other Ledas began to form their own culture, with special language (such as "clone club") and traditions (such as, say, impersonating one another).

Appiah sets out several aspects to building an identity in a social group—let's call that group "L." First, there must be some kind of identifiable *social conception* of the "kind of person" that is an L. Although it may be simplistic, prejudiced, and partly untrue, the social caricature or stereotype is necessary for the demarcation. These social conceptions often involve characteristics over which individuals have no control: female, Hispanic, gay, African, straight, male. People are often simply born into such descriptions. This is certainly true of the Ledas and Castors, who had no control over their unique origins.

Second, a name or label must evolve that describes the group. Although Appiah does not say it, to have a label connotes both a value judgment and a certain critical mass. There are no labels for vegetarians in Alabama because it is not important to most Alabamians or non-Alabamians to mark off such a group; whether or not one eats meat is low stakes, and there are not enough such people for it to matter to the majority. But there are still labels for "Yankee," "liberal," and "fundamentalist." For people originated by cloning, a powerful label already exists: "clone."

Third, individuals in the group must internalize the L label and apply it to themselves: "Yes, I am a bioethicist," for example. In *Orphan Black*, we see such internalization beginning early in season one, when Alison explains to Sarah in season one, episode three, "We're clones! We're someone's experiment ..." Although that particular expression of internalization is negative, another one, the Ledas' acceptance of their relationship and mutual support of one another, is more positive.

Fourth, there must be *a pattern of behavior* by others toward members of this L group. Often this is a bad pattern born in prejudice. Although we don't know for sure that such a prejudiced pattern of behavior would exist toward cloned people, *Orphan Black* certainly makes us feel that it would, for example, because of the similarity of its world to our own, as well as the fact that cloned humans remain a secret.

Appiah concludes, "Where a classification of people as Ls is associated with a *social conception* of Ls, some people *identify* as Ls, and people are sometimes *treated* as Ls, we have a paradigm of social identity that matters for ethical and political life."

So for the Ledas, they are classified (by those who know their secret) as clones, and in particular as products of Project

Leda; they come to identify with this description, and with their sisterhood; and they are treated differently (by Felix, Dyad, police officer Arthur Bell, and Topside) because of it. So for the Castors, they are classified (especially by the military) as clones, the products of Project Castor; they identify as a group; and they are treated by Dr. Coady and others differently from other members of the military, like Paul, as a result.

## KEEPING YOUR CLONES CLOSE

Although Appiah certainly was not thinking of clones in providing his analysis of social identity, I think his analysis perfectly fits clonal identity in *Orphan Black* and what might happen with cloned humans in reality.

Consider also another aspect of social identity not discussed by Appiah but that is very relevant to the Ledas and Castors, and which we touched on in the last chapter in the context of a group of two, twins: the pressures, within and without, to remain in the group and adhere to its standards. First, individuals who betray group identity feel guilty. There are some Americans who, when traveling abroad during times when sentiment runs high against America, claim they are New Zealanders or Canadians, then later feel guilty. Second, group members put social pressure to remain on individuals who try to break away. The social forces that bind individuals together in a group can act just as powerfully in preventing aberrant members from leaving. Mark discovers both of these things when he tries to abandon the Castors for Gracie, as does Alison when she initially rejects membership in the Leda sisterhood.

We see this in real-world groups all the time. The Pueblo tribe doesn't permit religious freedom among its members, who own property communally; a breakaway member who wants to adopt a different religion may lose his property rights. A young woman trying to break away from Mormon culture may face almost insurmountable pressures to stay in the fold. A Bengali girl rejecting an arranged marriage may be left on her own, with no means of support. African American teens who are perceived by their black peers as studying and reading what they consider "too much" may be accused of acting "too white"—they may be threatened with the withdrawal of group membership for violating assumed group standards.

Following Appiah's analysis of social identity in a group, it makes a profound difference whether individuals cloned from the same ancestor are raised in isolation with different families or together as a group. The Ledas feel these group pressures and exhibit these hallmarks of group identity despite having met only as adults; from what we have seen of the Castors, both factors appear intensified, given their upbringing. Whether the same would be true of cloned humans in our world—how they would see themselves, in either circumstance—is a fascinating question yet to be answered.

## CHAPTER 17

# Stealing and Swapping Identities

## *Twins and Clones*

*"If we're going to go road-tripping to steal some poor clone's iden-tity, then I've only got one demand: I get to choose the music."*
—Felix to Sarah, "Ruthless in Purpose and
Insidious in Method," season three, episode eight

**O**rphan Black opens with one person stealing the iden-tity of another, a theft facilitated by the remark-able fact that the victim looks exactly like the thief. Sarah Manning steals not only Elizabeth Childs' identity, but also her boyfriend, her job as a police detective, and her money.

The idea of stealing someone else's identity is not new. Ditching one's identity by taking over the identity of a better-situated person appeals to people who fantasize about a do-over in life. Although Sarah seems to be only in her late twenties, her life has taken some wrong turns. She left her daughter, Kira, in the care of Mrs. S one night and then did not return for ten months. She has dealt cocaine and stolen from others (she steals $15,000 worth of cocaine from Vic by assaulting him with an ashtray; she also steals Beth's purse, savings, apartment, and car). Although she puts up a brave front, by her own admission Sarah has been a lousy mother to Kira. Maybe being Beth Childs seemed easier than being Sarah Manning.

However, having identical clones around gives this theme a new twist. In fact, *Orphan Black* repeats this device of one sestra impersonating another throughout all three seasons. So Sarah impersonates Beth to help her sister clones; Helena impersonates the deceased Beth at the police station to spy on Sarah; Alison impersonates Sarah to Mrs. S to help Sarah earn back visitation of Kira (even though Kira doesn't buy it); Sarah impersonates Alison to interrogate Alison's husband, Donnie; Rachel impersonates Sarah to steal Kira; Sarah impersonates Rachel to steal Dyad's secrets; Cosima impersonates Alison at a political rally; and Rachel poses as Krystal to escape Dyad (while Krystal, put into a coma by Sarah and Felix, stands in for Rachel).

The sestras must constantly cover for each other by assuming each other's identities while one of them is off doing the real work of investigating why they were created and who is trying to kill them. But the sestras must also cover up when another Leda has impersonated them *without their consent*, as when Helena calls Paul as Sarah-playing-Beth and asks Paul to come get her. (Paul, we later learn, *did* know Beth was a clone, though he did not realize she was dead—and of course Sarah, Alison, and Cosima did not know how much Paul knew at the time.)

Philosophers like to carefully define their terms and to make distinctions. So here we should distinguish between *stealing* an identity and *swapping* identities. The first is involuntary and a kind of theft; the second, although it may deceive others, is not theft and presumes voluntary agreement between the two exchanging identities.

So let's discuss identity theft. What is so bad about it?

Well, we know from our own lives that when a thief uses our credit card to buy things for himself in our name, or obtains a new card for himself using our personal information, it can be quite destructive. In some of the worst cases of such identity theft, victims have been stuck with hundreds of thousands of dollars worth of debt they never incurred.

Stealing someone's identity is a very serious ethical breach. As the late ethicist James Rachels famously argued, controlling who knows what about us is a key to being a free, autonomous person, which is why the right to privacy is so important. But when someone is impersonating you, you lose all control over how "you" are presented to the world; all your efforts to build your good character can be quickly wiped out by an unscrupulous person. This also explains why identity theft is a crime; it can seriously harm someone's reputation as well as his or her financial resources.

One infamous 2007 case of identity theft involved then–college student Brittany Ossenfort, whose roommate Michelle became her unusually close friend. Michelle started dressing and wearing her hair like Brittany, which Brittany initially took as compliments. The two lived together like this for a year. But then police called Brittany one day, asking her to bail out "Brittany Ossenfort" from jail on charges of prostitution. After some more investigation, Brittany was shocked to learn that Michelle's legal name was Michael Phillips and she was transgender.

(A similar situation drove the plot of the 1992 movie *Single White Female*. In it, the imposter is not a transgender woman but a girl who, mourning the loss of her deceased twin, seeks out roommates like her twin, dresses and acts like them, and then, when disappointed by their inability to replace her sister, ends up killing them.)

Another famous case of real-life identity theft occurred in 2010 when twenty-six Israeli Mossad agents stole the identity of twenty-six ordinary people with clean, unremarkable profiles and, under their names, checked into a fancy hotel in Dubai. A high-ranking officer in Hamas, Mahmoud al-Mabhouh, was later found dead in his room in the same hotel, apparently assassinated. One of the people whose identity was stolen, Nicole McCabe, a pregnant Australian woman living in Israel, had a lot of trouble afterward establishing that she had not killed the Hamas leader.

## The Evil Twin and Identity Swaps in Literature and Myth

Literature and mythology abound with stories of an evil twin. When it is obvious that one twin is evil and the other good, the evil one is often identified via a physical difference—a goatee or scar or physical impairment of some sort. Think about how the "evil" Castor clone Rudy has a prominent facial scar, so we can easily tell him apart from "good" Mark, the Castor who marries Gracie. Given the precedent of this idea of a dark double, it's easy to see how clones—an unnatural version of twins— have come to be associated with things to be feared.

Often, in these evil-twin stories, one twin tricks or kills the other. Possibly this trope dates back to fears about primogeniture, where the firstborn inherited all the land while his twin, born several minutes later, got nothing. In the biblical story of Isaac's fraternal twins, Esau and Jacob, Jacob (the second born) and his mother conspire to deceive Isaac for Esau's inheritance. Biblical twins Pharez and Zarah, Jacob's grandsons, also fought over birthright (one's hand came out first and the midwife marked it with a scarlet thread, but then the hand was withdrawn and the other twin unexpectedly emerged, leading the twins and their descendants to fight over who was rightfully first). Romulus and Remus, legendary founders of Rome, are feuding twins, and in some versions of the myth, Romulus kills Remus in a power struggle.

Like the story of Esau and Jacob, where Jacob impersonates Esau to trick Isaac into bestowing his blessing on the wrong son, many stories of twins involve one twin assuming the identity of the other—sometimes with permission and sometimes not. Think of *The Parent Trap*, or Mark

Twain's *The Prince and the Pauper*, where identical boys or girls, usually with very different lives, pretend to be each other by mutual agreement. In Shakespeare's *Twelfth Night* and *The Comedy of Errors*, mistaken identities of twins (fraternal twins in *Twelfth Night* and identical twins in *The Comedy of Errors*) play major roles in attempted seduction, feigned madness, and accusations of infidelity.

In stories of evil twins, it is usually the evil twin who assumes, or steals, the identity of the good twin. The classic literary tale of such an identity theft is *The Man in the Iron Mask*, by Alexandre Dumas, based on Voltaire's writings, in which the identical twin of King Louis XIV of France is imprisoned in the Bastille for thirty-four years. In *A Stolen Life*, a 1946 remake of a 1939 British movie, after a boat accident involving both twins in which one drowns, the evil twin assumes the married life of the good twin.

---

In another brazen case of identity theft in Wichita, Kansas, a man left his house for a few months to care for his sick mother. While he was gone, another man and his wife moved into his house, used all the resident's credit cards to buy things, and even visited local police to inform them that the imposter was an undercover agent using the house and not to investigate any complaints of a new person in the house. The imposter and his wife were even able to take out a second mortgage on the house, using the real owner's documents.

But what happens when the identity thief is a person closely related to you? Your twin rather than a more easily discernable impersonator? The problem has already arisen in criminal cases where it cannot be established beyond a reasonable doubt that twin X did the crime rather than twin Y. In Malaysia in 2009, a judge spared two twins from execution because prosecutors could not prove which twin owned confiscated narcotics.

It's worth nothing that, had fingerprints of the crime-committing twin been available, being twins wouldn't have saved them. Contrary to popular thinking, identical twins actually have different fingerprints due to various factors: place in the uterus, random inactivation of the X chromosome, and even scarring. Epigenetics may further distinguish the fingerprints of twins, triplets, or even Leda clones (despite Cosima's claim early in season one that deceased clone Katja's fingerprints would be close enough to Beth's to come up as a match).

Of course, the problem of which twin committed a crime would be compounded if there were twelve copies of you. Let's say one of your fellow clones, who made less money than you did, often assumed your identity as a rich person, say, by charging things at your country club or using a fake ID with your name and picture on it to enter a health club. For judges and police officers, having twelve versions of the criminal's genotype walking around would obviously make finding the true criminal much more difficult. Likewise, if all of a set of twelve clones conspired to commit a crime, and deliberately used smoke screens to conceal the identity of the guilty person or confuse the police, the difficulty would increase exponentially.

The Ledas in *Orphan Black* have the opposite problem. Since the world does not know they are clones, one

Leda breaking the law would put all of them in danger—collectively, were their secret to get out and, individually, were any of them caught by the police in place of the actual criminal.

Fortunately, the importance of secrecy makes acts of impersonation less risky. Rachel can't easily go to the police to turn Sarah in for stealing Dyad secrets; how would she explain how Sarah had done it? And who would guess their suburban neighbor had been impersonated by her identical clone? So it's a handy plot device, despite the ethical issues—and one that certainly makes for exciting plots, not to mention a wonderful acting showcase for Tatiana Maslany's ability to play a character within a character.

## CHAPTER 18

# Clones and Free Will

*"Life is like a game of cards. The hand you are dealt is
determinism; the way you play it is free will."*
—Jawaharlal Nehru

So much of our personality and character is fixed by our
genes and our upbringing that, from the time of the
ancient Stoics and Epicureans, philosophers have speculated
as to whether free will exists or is just an illusion. Circumstances, also, can limit our sense of freedom: An intelligent,
fit child born to an upper-middle-class, white family with
loving parents has more freedom in life than a disabled child
born to a poor single mother with seven other children.

On top of the normal constraints on free will, people created by cloning would seem to have special problems. They have not only the determinism of their genes to contend with, but also the life of their ancestor. If this ancestor died from a genetic disease like early-onset Alzheimer's disease, is it a foregone conclusion that the clone would also die this way? Suppose, too, the ancestor was a talented singer. Would the cloned woman have any choice in also becoming a singer? Certainly expectations would be great that she would, as we have discussed. So would she really be free to shun singing and instead become a nun or an elementary school teacher?

This question of free will also appears, if in an understated way, in *Orphan Black*. After arranging Helena's capture and imprisonment, Dr. Coady explains to her why she is so valuable: "Helena, you have overcome so much: your upbringing, your biology, your fate. This makes you quite a special case. We are going to find out how." Of course, Helena is so special and free that she also escapes her captors. So perhaps there is room in cloned people for free will, after all.

## BASIC PHILOSOPHICAL POSITIONS ON FREE WILL

Thinking in the history of philosophy about free will has revolved around five basic stances: fatalism, determinism, indeterminism, incompatibilism, and compatibilism.

Within the last, compatibilism, there are also significant variations.

*Fatalism* holds that no matter what you decide, certain key events in your future are fixed. Oedipus might try not to sleep with his mother or kill his father and sail away to avoid his fate, but when he returns many years later, he does exactly that. Similarly, if you have certain autosomal dominant hereditary diseases, such as Huntington's disease, then—absent a miraculous cure in the coming decades— you are going to get this terrible disease.

Clearly some things are fixed, no matter how hard we try to avoid them. We are mortal. Our bodies age and our minds decline. By age sixty, we will likely look a lot like our mother or father, or a combination of the two, at that age, so if both were thirty pounds overweight and if mom's dad was bald and dad was bald, you are likely be thirty pounds overweight and bald as well. We can fight these processes, but only so far.

However, just because some things in life are fixed doesn't mean that everything is. Fatalism is often confused with *determinism*, the view that nothing happens randomly and every event has a cause. Fatalism focuses on causes outside our control, such as a driver who runs a red light and hits our car.

Determinism is an operational thesis in science and ordinary life: If a tree suddenly falls on a playground in California, we assume something caused the tree to fall, such as water-soaked earth and strong winds. If my tooth starts to hurt, I look for the cause of that new phenomenon;

perhaps something I have recently eaten has caused this change. If I cannot discover the cause on my own, I will see a dentist.

*Indeterminism* holds that some events are uncaused. In the free will debate, it then equates "uncaused" with "free." This view is associated with existentialism and especially the French philosopher Jean Paul Sartre, who wrote that humans are "condemned to be free," meaning that free will is a burden that inauthentic people seek to escape.

*Compatibilism* holds that determinism can be true and we can still have a range of free will. *Incompatibilism* claims that free will and determinism are incompatible. Defenders of compatibilism include the English empiricist David Hume and the modern philosopher Robert Kane.

In the case of my hurt tooth, I could be fatalistic and assume I have no control over my teeth, or I could decide that I have a choice and try to discover the cause. Even if something has injured my tooth, compatibilists think I still have some control over my life and body. If the tooth is broken, I can choose to have it fixed.

Compatibilism sees indeterminists' demand that free actions have no causal antecedents as unjustified. For compatibilists, free decisions do not occur in a vacuum; they just proceed from our desires and decisions.

Indeterminists might retort, "But can you choose your own desires? Who shaped them? If they are not self-chosen, you are unfree."

Suppose that I recall eating hard candy the day before the pain began in my tooth. Now I infer that eating the hard candy may have caused my tooth to break. Suppose I then vow, to save my teeth, to never eat hard candy again. Am I then free?

Some determinists say I am not because I cannot choose to like hard candy or not and cannot choose whether I want to avoid pains in my teeth. These are just "given" desires. As an adult, I like sweets and I also dislike pain in my tooth. If I must be able to choose such desires to be free, then I am not free.

On the other hand, what most people want from free will is not the ability to choose their desires from a buffet of possible desires, but instead to be able to act to satisfy the desires they have. I'd like to keep my teeth and eat hard candy, but if I can't do both, I can decide to do one or the other. If I can do that, I'm free enough for me.

In general, by the time we arrive as adults, most of our desires, such as our sexual orientation, are fixed, and not only are we not free to change them, it is not necessarily good or desirable to do so. What we want, when we say we wish to be free, compatibilists assert, is a non-fatalistic open future where, say, our desire to take a walk in the evening is not thwarted by external events beyond our control. If a violent storm begins and we cannot walk, we are not as free as we thought—but even then, if we are so foolish, we are free to take the risk. In the same way, we are free to determine if eating hard candy has caused our teeth to break, and to refrain from eating such candy in the future.

So when Helena is caged by Tomas, or imprisoned in a cell in the desert by Dr. Coady and the Castors, she has little freedom because she cannot act on her desires to immediately escape, to eat what she wants, and so on. She is unfree because external events control her range of choices.

But she still possesses some small range of free actions, as evidenced by her hoarding of butter packets in Mexico and her eventual escape from both jailers. In the same way, even though Sarah is strapped down to a gurney before her impending oophorectomy, Cosima arms Sarah with a gun that shoots a sharpened pencil into Rachel's eye, giving Sarah a triumphant free action.

## CLONED HUMANS AND FREE WILL

So what choices do Ledas and Castors have? First, let's reiterate something we established early on in this book: Clones are not zombies. Zombies have no souls, hence, they have no free will.

Second, Ledas and Castors are persons. If persons have free will, then human clones have free will.

Third, notice that genetic essentialism—which asserts that "Genes 'R' Us" for all people (clones included)—is a version of fatalism, one that puts all the weight of formation of character on what we inherit biologically. Yet we already know that genetic essentialism is false, because our environment affects the expression of our inherited genes. So we can toss genetic essentialism out the window, which allows free action to enter.

## PSYCHOLOGICAL UNFREEDOM

When we move from genetics to psychology, the discussion about free will shifts from genes to expectations and reinforcement. Seminal psychological thinkers like Sigmund Freud and B. F. Skinner assert that although humans may be free or unfree in other senses, in their emotional and mental states, they are completely determined and unfree because of the influence of their parents or the conditioning of their upbringing. It is here that cloned humans may also be especially vulnerable to charges of being unfree.

For example, most of us in early childhood want to please our parents, whether our parents' desire for us is athletic prowess, financial success, or educational attainment. Suppose, as a clone, you only have one parent, your ancestor, a great piano player, and she desires that you learn to play the piano. How free would you be to resist?

One problem here stems from only having the one parent. The more control a person has over a child, the less free the child. This is why some people wish to homeschool their child—because they want complete control over how and what their child learns. This is also why others object to homeschooling—because they want to ensure that all children get a broad education.

Let's imagine that all of a cloned child's "mothers"—the genetic ancestor, the egg donor, the surrogate, and the raising mother—were both part of her life and conspired to urge her to play the piano. Assume also the child is homeschooled by one of these women. Would the girl have much of a chance of resisting learning to play the piano?

Probably not.

Okay, let's make it even worse. Instead of homeschooling, suppose that a twelve-year-old cloned child is sent to the John Lennon and Yoko Ono Magnet School for the Performing Arts. Suppose her ancestor is Beyoncé. Suppose every child and teacher at this school knows that she is a clone of Beyoncé. At this school, she meets a twelve-year-old boy whose last name is Mozart and who made his debut on the piano at age four, reinforcing the idea that cloned children are obligated to develop their God-given talents.

Here the child is faced with the expectations not only of her ancestor parent, but also her entire school and, quite possibly, her entire community. Could that mini-Beyoncé really resist if the voice teacher asked her to sing? To try out for a role in the upcoming school musical?

Chances are very high that a cloned child, so long as she and those around her knew she was cloned, would enjoy a smaller range of free acts than a normal child. I don't see any way around this conclusion, unless you were to deny that the reason to clone Beyoncé is for her most well-known qualities.

Despite this, some wiggle room for free will remains. After all, not every daughter of a Baptist minister becomes a devout Baptist—and, in fact, the wild minister's daughter who revolts against her father is downright cliché.

Amazingly and famously, birth order may even be important to the development of personality and to how much free will children exhbit. Firstborn children notoriously seek to please their parents. Less time is spent on second-born, who tend to be contrarians, partly in order to get attention. After the French Revolution, firstborns famously favored not executing aristocrats and preserving the social order, while almost all the second-borns (who were in control) favored sending them to the guillotine to start over with a new social order.

The most dramatic diminution of free will in *Orphan Black* is seen in the Castors. Because they were raised together and in isolation, and for a specific purpose, their range of free actions seems much smaller than the Ledas, who at least were raised (mostly) by normal families and only monitored, not controlled. So we can't imagine the Castors training to be cellists or flutists in an orchestra, nor can we imagine them wanting to be school counselors. They are human "action figures"—primed for quick strikes, taking orders, and acting like a military platoon on patrol in enemy territory.

## ELBOW ROOM

The philosopher Daniel Dennett, famous for his writings on free will, argues that "the kind of freedom worth having" does not require us to choose everything (our desires, our parents, whether to be born, etc.) but simply requires us to have some real choice in our actions, which he refers to as having some "elbow room" to act.

Based on having inherited genes from one ancestor, and the expectations by those who raise them based on that ancestor's genes, cloned children may be less free than normal children. (It is also true that similar parental expectations on children created sexually might equally limit any child's range of free action.) But even cloned children have some elbow room, such as rebelling against expectations thrust on them. It is also theoretically possible that a child cloned from a certain kind of ancestor might be as free, or even *more* free, than normal. Suppose the ancestor was a notorious freethinker, rebel, or contrarian. And suppose the child's creators went to great pains not to manipulate the child into any outcome. In that case, it would be very interesting to see what occurred.

As some philosophers have emphasized, what is most important for free will is degrees of self-awareness. In one sense, this is the whole point of most forms of psychotherapy: to give you insight into why you feel and act the way you do, say, from a desire to please your hard-to-please dad. Only by becoming aware of the forces controlling your actions, therapists say, can you choose to go against them or continue to let them control you.

In the same way, a self-aware Leda such as Rachel has more choices and more freedom than Krystal Goderitch, a non-self-aware clone. Though the other Ledas, such as Cosima, Helena, Sarah, and Alison, became aware of their origins later in life, the events of the show are a testament to their free choices ever since.

Deep down, anyone can resist expectations placed on them. Once adults are on their own, especially if they achieve insight through reflection and counseling (or, say, discovery of their origin as a clone), anyone can be free.

## CHAPTER 19

# Helena, Freud, Henrik, and Foucault

*"You should not threaten babies."*
—Helena to nannies in Henrik's compound, "Insolvent
Phantom of Tomorrow," season three, episode nine

Why do we love Helena? Why are we always so eager to see what she does next? Why is Helena the kick-ass friend we'd all love to have when, like Donnie and Alison, you unexpectedly have to face drug dealers?

We love her because she is a survivor, despite past abuse. In the terms of modern positive psychology, she is resilience embodied. She has been knocked down, but she rebounds. The Castors waterboard her, but she endures. She is tough, an Amazon, with a soft exterior and insides of steel. She can quote Nietzsche: "What does not kill me makes me stronger."

Helena is a female Jason Bourne, an assassin trained by Proletheans Tomas and Maggie Chen to kill with a sniper rifle, a knife, and her own hands. Like Bourne, when her trainers turn against her, Helena must use her lethal skills to survive.

Helena is a less mature Lisbeth Salander—not a woman of the world and quite naïve about technology, but like Lisbeth someone who will stand up for her sisters, especially to abusive men. If you are with her, she has your back. When she intones ominously, "You should not threaten babies," we know that neither the women at Henrik's compound nor the sleazy drug dealers ripping off Donnie know what is about to happen—the soft, purring Ukrainian kitten is about to morph into a ninja-assassin killer who takes no prisoners. Threaten her babies and you die.

Helena is a Ukrainian version of *Homeland*'s Carrie Mathison. Both Helena and Carrie struggle against their inner demons, refusing to be constrained by social conventions and, despite what others think of them, obsessively pursuing their own goals, often resorting to deception to do so.

If Helena were a *Dungeons & Dragons* character, her alignment would be chaotic good.

Helena is all Freudian id. She does not hide her passions: for food, for alcohol, for love. She is childlike in her neediness.

Her clone sisters Alison and Sarah serve here as instructive contrasts. In Freudian terms, Alison is the superego of the group, the obsessive-compulsive, suburban soccer mom for whom everything must run on schedule. Helena is her primal opposite. Meanwhile, in discovering her clone sisters and unique origins, Sarah has been transformed from punk con artist to the Ledas' ego, their prefrontal lobe. Sarah's strength, bravery, and cunning make her their leader, deftly negotiating between and using the best parts of Helena's id and Alison's superego. Sarah soon realizes that Helena is a weapon that she can suppress or unleash: "If you don't obey, I'll sic Helena on you," Sarah tells Dr. Leekie. And Leekie knows she can. Helena is rather like a dangerous beast that Sarah has tamed, thanks to the connection Helena feels to Sarah as her in utero twin.

If Rachel Duncan, raised like the Castor men as a tool for her creators, fits the trope of the evil twin, Helena is only half-evil. "Helena is not a monster," Mrs. S tells Sarah. "Just trained to be a killer." Helena has both good and bad in her. She has been damaged, but the love of Sarah, and Sarah's daughter, Kira, can redeem her.

We also see Helena's goodness when she plays with children, and more important, protects them—not only the kids of the Prolethean farm but especially Kira and Alison's two children. These scenes also allow us to see Helena's childlike immaturity, which is what allows her to relate to children but also indicates that Helena is still unformed, capable of becoming more damaged but also of being healed by love.

It is also instructive to look at Helena and her plotlines in *Orphan Black* in terms of the twentieth-century French philosopher Michel Foucault, who famously argued that modern institutions such as prisons and mental hospitals exist to control their inmates. For Foucault, the purpose of *every* institution in the modern State, from the military to elementary schools to the police to colleges to social workers, is to control citizens. Accordingly, such institutions abhor deviance above all else, especially in individuals who do not bend to their control.

We know little of Foucault's childhood, other than that he described himself as a truant and contrarian. We know he was gay and that his sadistic father beat him. Like Helena with the nuns, Foucault learned to hide his true character and to understand that the world was against him.

For Foucault, all institutions control people and their bodies in four basic ways: *spatially*, in directing how far apart bodies exist and whether they intermingle; *organically*, by forcing bodies into "normal" activities and suppressing "abnormal" actions; *genetically*, by controlling the evolution over time of bodies and their offspring; and *combinatorily*, in dictating when bodies can legitimately come together.

Take elementary schools. Children who formerly were as active as they desired must learn to be quiet and behave in concert with other children. Those who cannot adapt—say, those with diagnoses of attention deficit disorder—must be sent to a "special" school or given medication to make them conform. Most important, students must learn to obey the teacher, who must be in control of the students or be fired.

For Foucault, knowledge and language function to control, especially in the way they categorize the Other. In his

*History of Madness*, Foucault describes how labels of mental abnormality—labels such as "witch," "bitch," "whore," "crazy," and "lesbian"—functioned historically to control women in particular. In contrast to real mental illness, which has a biological basis, for Foucault many forms of madness are socially constructed to control deviance. (This work fueled libertarian critiques of psychiatry, especially the 1962 book *The Myth of Mental Illness* by Hungarian psychiatrist Thomas Szasz.)

In sum, for Foucault, things we take for granted as liberating or natural, such as going to school, having parents, or attending religious services, are actually socially constructed mechanisms for suppressing deviance, controlling individuals, and shaping how sexuality can be appropriately expressed. In the modern world, institutions strive to create pliant, docile bodies that must be trained, observed, and, above all else, obedient.

Topside and the Dyad Corporation's treatment of the Ledas perfectly reflects Foucault's conception of the world: Each cloned sister has a *monitor* to observe her and, if necessary, help these organizations kill her, as happened with the Leda clones in Helsinki.

But we see Foucault's ideas most keenly in Helena's story. Helena was raised in a convent orphanage in Ukraine that the official *Orphan Black* site describes as "oppressive and harsh." Like prisons, orphanages are often some of the most controlling places on Earth, and in Helena's orphanage, religion, with its promise of Heaven and threat of Hell, was likely used to manipulate her behavior. The time she spent after, with Tomas and the Proletheans, and then at Henrik's compound, must have been, in many ways, similar: subjected to religious doctrine aimed at controlling her behavior, and punished (and even physically caged) when doctrine failed.

When Helena and later Sarah are imprisoned somewhere in a Mexican desert in season three, we see more evidence of Foucault's themes. Everything about Helena is monitored and controlled. But her training and previous institutionalization have prepared her to survive this experience. She notices small things inside her cell. She cleverly hides butter and learns the routine of the guards, down to seconds, then brilliantly plots, waits, kills, and escapes.

Season two's story line, and the positioning of Henrik as a foil to Helena, has particular resonance with Foucault. Charismatic Henrik and the New World Proletheans take obvious inspiration from religious cults, such as Jim Jones and his Peoples Temple cult in Jonestown, Guyana, or fundamentalist Mormon groups in southern Utah made notorious by Jon Krakauer in *Under the Banner of Heaven*. So we are not surprised that, when his daughter Gracie opposes him, Henrik's syrupy words to her about hearing God in the whispered silences turn to sadistic action when he literally silences Gracie for not alerting him about Helena's escape by sewing Gracie's mouth shut.

Henrik personifies everything Foucault thought was wrong with religion and hierarchical institutions. These institutions and the men who run them serve to oppress women and minorities, regiment them, control them, and bend them to their will. Everything that Henrik says to Gracie and to Mark, his adopted son, serves to increase Henrik's power in the social hierarchy. Everything he does to Helena—most obviously, harvesting her eggs and fertilizing them with his own sperm, making him the father of the divinely ordered special children they'll produce—is calculated to boost this power, too, even at the expense of contradicting his cult's original ideals.

That is because Henrik, as opposed to Tomas, is not really motivated by religious belief or piety. The compound and its ideology is *really all about him*. Religion here is just a ruse for controlling other people. That is why, when Gracie opposes him, while remaining true to the cult's original ideals, she must be punished—and when the punishment does not work, why she must go.

Tomas and Henrik both brainwash their respective Prolethean followers to hear the Eternal in silence, which amounts to accepting everything that Tomas or Henrik want. We know this because, under Tomas, they abhorred anything about assisted reproduction, mimicking the current position of the Catholic Church; that is why they kidnapped Helena, to destroy her as a spawn of Satan. But then Henrik makes them abruptly reverse their position, which is where the "New World" Proletheans depart from Tomas' Old World cult.

Why? Well, we know that Tomas and Henrik clashed over this belief. We know that Henrik is evil because he not only has Tomas murdered but has Mark do so. Only a leader confident in the silence and complicity of his followers would act this way. Henrik is smug, arrogant, and ambitious, all under a false coat of humility and piety.

We know this type.

Helena is correct when she tells Gracie that Henrik sees young women as his "brood mares." In his own mind and supreme narcissism, Henrik is the spiritual and physical instrument of God. Henrik tried once to reproduce himself, resulting in a son, Abel, who died shortly after birth. Now God has sent Helena to him, with her special healing powers, and it is only right that Henrik's sperm should be the male element in the new, divinely ordered Super Beings to come.

Although the Old and New World Proletheans are at opposite ends of one spectrum, ideologically, when it comes to their stance on clones, they both operate the same way: Both groups believe their higher end justifies anything. So the Old World Proletheans train Helena to hunt down and kill her sister-clones. Under Henrik, the New World Proletheans accept Tomas' murder, the kidnapping and rape of Helena (because forced insemination is, indeed, a kind of rape), the false imprisonment without judge or trial of Gracie in a barn stall with steel bars, and the death or banishment of anyone who stands in their way. After all—and it is worth repeating—Henrik barbarically *sews together his daughter's lips* as punishment for opposing him. Afterward, when Helena comforts Gracie, she tells her that the sadistic nuns did the same to her.

The Neolutionists are no different. They, too, believe their higher end justifies their actions, particularly when it comes to monitoring and controlling the Ledas.

For Foucault, resistance to domination takes a plurality of forms, and it is often in resisting such domination that humans become truly free. So Helena, in resisting the control of Protheans, Neolutionists, Dyad, and Topside, breaks the mold and becomes free. And that, I suspect, is the true reason we love Helena: More than any other character in *Orphan Black*, Helena is free.

## CHAPTER 20

# Top Five Ideas for Future *Orphan Black* Episodes

O*rphan Black* has been renewed for at least a fourth season and hopefully will run for many more. We know new things are coming. For instance, the official *Orphan Black* comic book informed us in August 2015 that one of the sestras from the Helsinki Leda pod, Veera Suominen, did not die when Topside ordered them destroyed in a fire.

Some things I hope will not change: the Canadian feel of the show, where we have occasional violence but not the gross violence of American shows; the ambiguity of the city, which could be in the north of America or the south of Canada (even though everything is actually filmed in Toronto); Kathryn Alexandre, perhaps the greatest and most unappreciated understudy ever, who constantly doubles as Tatiana Maslany in key scenes where the Ledas interact (shots are often filmed with Maslany and Alexandre, then Maslany does the take again as the clone that Alexandre was playing). So where could the plot go in future episodes? Obviously, anywhere its creators want, but in case they run out of ideas, here are five, based on the science of cloning and what has worked well in other medical and science fiction dramas.

## 1. ONE CLONE SACRIFICES HEROICALLY FOR ANOTHER

Because the Ledas and Castors are genetically 99 percent identical, they are perfect donors for surgical exchange; their immune systems will not reject one another's tissue, blood, or bone. Accordingly, one future plot could involve one sestra sacrificing something to save another Leda's life. This could be as simple as a transplant or a transfusion of blood, skin, or bone marrow, but could involve much more, such as a piece of a liver, a kidney, or a cornea. If an otherwise healthy clone were dying or brain dead, her organs could be transplanted to save another sestra.

Think of Jodi Picoult's *My Sister's Keeper*, where parents of a dying girl decide to have what bioethicists call a "savior sibling," a second child who is a good match for his or her older sibling and who can be used as a source of bone marrow, a transplanted kidney, or a bit of liver. The tension in the family and the conflict of interests create riveting bioethics drama.

This basic idea has many variations, but one that has worked well historically in fiction is for a villain, such as Rachel, to be redeemed by sacrificing herself to save another. Or, if a Castor were to sacrifice himself for a Leda, it might forge new bonds between the two groups of clones.

Twins in the real world often sacrifice for each other medically and seem to do so quite willingly; as mentioned, the first kidney transplant occurred in 1954 between two adult male twins. The special bond between genetically identical individuals seems to play a part in encouraging one twin to help the other, even at great risk to herself.

## 2. A NEW POD OF CLONES IS DISCOVERED

Topside and the Dyad Corporation created two sets of clones that we know of (albeit from the same genetic ancestor); who knows what else they've been up to? A whole new set of clones might emerge—and perhaps this time, someone non-white will be its ancestor.

What additional storytelling resonance might emerge from dealing with a group of, say, Asian women in their twenties living in Shanghai who discover they are clones? What differences could it make that they were raised in a non-democratic regime? (We already know rumors that in China, convicted murderers who are the right organ match for important Chinese officials needing an organ transplant are sometimes executed early and with surgical efficiency to preserve their organs.) What difference would it make if the level of surveillance and control tolerated by citizens were much greater than in North America? Worship of ancestors is a strong part of Confucianism. Would this make a difference in how the cloned women feel about being descended from the same ancestor?

## 3. CLONES ARE DISCOVERED WHO MUST BE RESCUED

Perhaps Dyad has been very busy and some new teenage clones are discovered. The new clones are being raised in a remote place and are approaching the age where they can be exploited either for organs, as in the 2005 movie *The Island* or the 2005 novel *Never Let Me Go*, or perhaps for scientific research.

A rescue mission could be a great opportunity for the Castors and Ledas to work together. Now approaching age thirty, they might see the teenagers as "their children" and work to help them become self-aware and resist their intended fate.

## 4. A CLONE IS THREATENED WITH A TRIAL AND IMPRISONMENT

As we've seen, identical twins have in fact escaped conviction when a prosecutor could not prove beyond a reasonable doubt that one twin did the crime and not another. If a Leda were prosecuted for a crime, her sisters could help get her off, perhaps by providing an alibi. ("Judge, she couldn't have done it—look, she was caught by this ATM camera all the way across town at the time of the murder!") Maybe Alison gets caught selling drugs, or Dyad and Topside frame Sarah for something to get her out of the way. Whatever crime the Leda is charged with, her sestras could make proving that she did the crime "beyond a reasonable doubt" very difficult.

## 5. HUMANZEES ARE CREATED

Using cloning techniques and genetic manipulation, such as with the CRISPR techniques previously discussed, the Dyad Corporation creates a *humanzee*—a part-human, part-chimpanzee (or other animal) hybrid. Think not just Olivier's tail, but a whole human-chimp hybrid. Think a Castor with super upper-body strength. The Ledas or Castors might then need to rescue him from the evil scientists or evil generals.

Of course, none of this or all of this may happen in future episodes of *Orphan Black*. That's the exciting part about the show—its basis in cloning, realistic science, and bioethics means that not only can it grow in so many different ways, but new plots can be driven by the latest breakthroughs in medicine and science as they arise, commenting on the same issues our society is grappling with in real life.

# References

## CHAPTER 2

Cameron, Nigel, quoted in Deborah Sharpe and Lori Sharn. "Big Questions for Humanity." *USA Today*, April 1, 1997.

Kass, Leon. "The Wisdom of Repugnance." *New Republic*, June 2, 1997, 17–26.

McIntosh, Kerry Lynn. *Human Cloning: Four Fallacies and Their Legal Consequences.* New York: Cambridge University Press, 2013.

## CHAPTER 3

Fukuyama, Francis. "Human Nature and the Reconstruction of Social Order." *The Atlantic Monthly* 283, no. 5 (May 1999).

McCormick, Richard A. "Should We Clone Humans? Wholeness, Individuality, Reverence." *The Christian Century* 110, no. 33 (November 1993).

Nakasone, Ronald. "Buddhist Perspectives on Human Cloning." In *Ethical Issues in Human Cloning: Cross-Disciplinary Perspectives*, edited by Michael Brannigan. New York: Seven Bridges Press, 2001.

National Institutes of Health. *Report of the Human Embryo Research Panel.* September 1994.

Phillips, Adam. "Sameness Is All." In *Clones and Clones: Facts and Fantasies about Human Cloning*, by Martha C Nussbaum and Cass R. Sunstein. New York: Norton, 1999.

## CHAPTER 5

Kolata, Gina. "Researchers Clones Embryos of Human in Fertility Effort." *New York Times*, October 26, 1993, A1.

Kuhn, Thomas. *The Structure of Scientific Revolutions*. Chicago: University of Chicago Press, 1962.

Park, Alice. *The Stem Cell Hope: How Stem Cell Medicine Can Change Our Lives*. New York. Penguin, 2011.

Rorvik, David M. *In His Image: The Cloning of a Man*. New York: Lippincott, 1978.

Sang-Hun, Choe. "Disgraced Cloning Expert Convicted in South Korea." *New York Times*, October 26, 2009, A12.

Schrotenboer, Brent. "Fetal Stem Cells and the Sports Heroes They Revitalized." *USA Today*, May 19, 2015, http://www.usatoday.com/story/sports/2015/05/18/fetal-stem-cells-gordie-howe-john-brodie-tijuana-stroke-stemedica/27501717/.

Silver, Lee. *Remaking Eden*. New York: Avon Books, 1997.

Wilson, E. O. *Naturalist*. Washington, DC: Island Press, 1994.

## CHAPTER 6

Centers for Disease Control. "Bovine Spongiform Encephalopathy (BSE), or Mad Cow Disease." Last modified February 6, 2015, accessed September 7, 2015, http://www.cdc.gov/prions/bse/.

CNN. "Mad Cow Disease Fast Facts." Last modified June 9, 2015, accessed September 7, 2015, http://www.cnn.com/2013/07/02/health/mad-cow-disease-fast-facts/.

Pence, Gregory. "Europe and Mad Cow Disease." In *Designer Food: Mutant Harvest or Breadbasket of the World?* Lanham, MD: Rowman & Littlefield, 2001.

Pence, Gregory. *Re-Creating Medicine: Ethical Issues at the Frontiers of Medicine*. Lanham, MD: Rowman & Littlefield, 2000.

Sheils, Paul G. et al. "Analysis of Telomere Length in Dolly, a Sheep Derived by Nuclear Transfer." *Cloning* 1, no. 2 (1999): 119–25.

Taylor-Werner, Hermes. "Medicine's Wild West—Unlicensed Stem-Cell Clinics in the United States." *New England Journal of Medicine* 373 (2015): 985–87.

## CHAPTER 7

Annas, George, and Sherman Elias. *Genomic Messages: How the Evolving Science of Genetics Affects Our Health, Families and Future.* New York: HarperOne, 2015.

Bronson, Diana, Hope Shand, and Jim Thomas, eds. *Earth Grab: Geopiracy, the New Biomasters, and Capturing Climate Genes.* Oxford, England: Pambazuka Press, 2011.

Ginsberg, Alexandra Jane et al. *Synthetic Aesthetics: Investigating Synthetic Biology's Designs on Nature.* Cambridge, MA: MIT Press, 2014.

Kaebnick, G., M. Gusmano, and T. Murray. *Synthetic Future.* Special edition of the *Hastings Center Report* 44, no. 6 (2014).

Maxmen, Amy. "The Genesis Engine." *WIRED*, August 2015, http://www.wired.com/2015/07/crispr-dna-editing-2/.

Rasmussen, Steen et al., eds. *Protocells: Bridging Nonliving and Living Matter: Implications of Creating Life in the Laboratory.* Cambridge, MA: MIT Press, 2009.

Shapiro, Beth. *How to Clone a Mammoth: The Science of De-Extinction.* Princeton, NJ: Princeton University Press, 2015.

Stiglitz, Joseph. *The Price of Inequality: How Today's Divided Society Endangers Our Future.* New York: Norton, 2012.

Windsor, Matt. "'Holy Guanine, Batman!' Superheroes and Genetic Genius at the Frontiers of Science." *UAB: The Mix, Stories and Insights from UAB Research,* July 9, 2015, https://www.uab.edu/news/innovation/item/6283-holy-guanine-batman-superheroes-and-genetic-genius-at-the-frontiers-of-science.

## CHAPTER 8

Carroll, Amy E. "A Review of Recent Decisions of the United States Court of Appeals for the Federal Circuit." *American University Law Review* 44, Summer 1995.

*Diamond v. Chakrabarty,* 447 U.S. 303 (1980).

Eisenberg, Rebecca S. "Genetics and the Law: The Ethical, Legal, and Social Implications of Genetic Technology and Biomedical Ethics: Intellectual Property at the Public-Private Divide: The Case of Large-Scale DNA Sequencing." *University of Chicago Law School Roundtable* 3, no. 557 (1996).

Hanson, Mark J. "Religious Voices in Biotechnology: The Case of Gene Patenting." Special supplement of the *Hastings Center Report*, November–December, 1997.

Kass, Leon. "Patenting Life." *Commentary* 72, no. 6 (December 1981).

Lacy, Patricia A. "Gene Patenting: Universal Heritage vs. Reward for Human Effort." *Oregon Law Review* 77, Summer 1998.

Land, Richard D., and C. Ben Mitchell. "Patenting Life: No." *First Things* 63 (May 1996).

Levins, Richard, and Richard Lewontin. *The Dialectical Biologist.* Cambridge, MA: Harvard University Press, 1985.

Merz, Jon. "Disease Gene Patents: Overcoming Unethical Constraints on Clinical Laboratory Medicine." *Clinical Chemistry* 45, no. 3 (1999): 327.

Miller, Courtney J. "Comment: Patent Law and Human Genomics." *Capital University Law Review* 26 (1997): 893.

Mills, Claudia. "Patenting Life." *Report from the Center for Philosophy and Public Policy* 5, no. 1 (Winter 1985).

Nelkin, Dorothy, and M. Susan Lindee, *The DNA Mystique: The Gene as a Cultural Icon.* New York: W. H. Freeman & Company, 1995.

Ossorio, Pilar. "Legal and Ethical Issues in Biotechnology Patenting." In *A Companion to Genethics: Blackwell Companions to Philosophy*, edited by Justine Burley and John Harris, 408–19. Oxford: Blackwell Publishers, 2002.

Rifkin, Jeremy. *The Biotech Century.* New York: Tarcher, 1999.

Roberts, Leslie. "NIH Gene Patents: Round Two." *Science* 255, no. 5047 (1992): 912–13.

Shiva, Vandana. "Piracy through Patents: The Second Coming of Columbus." In *Biopiracy: The Plunder of Nature and Knowledge*, 1–6. Boston: South End Press, 1997.

Specter, Michael. "Decoding Iceland." *The New Yorker*, January 18, 1999.

## CHAPTER 9

Diamond, Jared. *Guns, Germs, and Steel: The Fates of Human Societies*. New York: Norton, 1997.

Kevles, Daniel. *In the Name of Eugenics: Genetics and the Uses of Human Heredity*. New York: Knopf, 1998.

Lacey, Robert. *Ford: The Men and the Machine*. New York: Little, Brown, 1987.

Mayell, Hillary. "Genghis Khan a Prolific Lover, DNA Data Implies." *National Geographic News*, February 14, 2003, http://news.nationalgeographic.com/news/2003/02/0214_030214_genghis.html.

Muller, Hermann J. *Out of the Night: A Biologist's View of the Future*. New York: Vanguard Press, 1935.

Parens, Erik, and Paul S. Appelbaum, eds. *The Genetics of Intelligence: Ethics and the Conduct of Trustworthy Research*, Special issue, *Hastings Center Report*, September/October 2015.

Pinker, Steven. *The Better Angels of Our Nature: Why Violence Has Declined*. New York: Viking, 2011.

Rachels, James. *Created from Animals: The Moral Implications of Darwinism*. Oxford, England: Oxford University Press, 1990.

Rawls, John. *A Theory of Justice*. Cambridge: Harvard University Press, 1974.

Stein, Rob. "Cloning Your Dog, for a Mere $100,000." *National Public Radio*, September 30, 2015, http://www.npr.org/sections/health-shots/2015/09/30/428927516/cloning-your-dog-for-a-mere-100-000.

*Wikipedia*, s.v. "Compulsory Sterilisation in Sweden." Last modified August 14, 2015, https://en.wikipedia.org/wiki/Compulsory_sterilisation_in_Sweden.

## CHAPTER 10

Bouchard, Thomas et al. "Sources of Human Psychological Differences: The Minnesota Study of Twins Reared Apart." *Science* 250, no. 4978 (1990): 223–28.

Landau, Elaine. *Joined at Birth: The Lives of Conjoined Twins*. New York: Grolier, 1997.

Nelson, Charles A., Nathan A. Fox, and Charles H. Zeanah. *Romania's Abandoned Children: Deprivation, Brain Development, and the Struggle for Recovery*. Cambridge, MA: Harvard University Press, 2014.

Quigley, Christine. *Conjoined Twins: An Historical, Biological and Ethical Issues Encyclopedia*. Jefferson, NC: McFarland & Company, 2003.

Wright, Lawrence. *Twins: And What They Tell Us About Who We Are*. New York: Wiley, 1997.

## CHAPTER 11

Gould, Stephen Jay. "Dolly's Fashion and Louis's Passion." *Natural History*, June 1997.

Wu, Cynthia. *Chang and Eng Reconnected: The Original Siamese Twins in American Culture*. Philadelphia: Temple University Press, 2012.

## CHAPTER 12

Colapinto, John. *As Nature Made Him: The Boy Who Was Raised as a Girl*. New York: HarperCollins, 2000.

Consortium on the Management of Disorders of Sex Development. *Clinical Guidelines for the Management of Disorders of Sex Development in Childhood*. Rohnert Park, CA: Intersex Society of North America, 2006.

Dowd, Maureen. "Between Torment and Happiness." *New York Times*, April 26, 2011.

Eugenides, Jeffrey. *Middlesex*. New York: Picador, 2002.

Foucault, Michel. *The History of Sexuality, Vol. 1: An Introduction*. Translated by Robert Hurley. New York: Vintage, 1990.

Mohr, Richard D. *Gays/Justice: A Study of Ethics, Society, and Law*. New York: Columbia University Press, 1988.

Sax, L. "How Common Is Intersex? A Response to Ann Fausto-Sterling." *Journal of Sex Research* 39, no. 3 (2002): 174–78.

## CHAPTER 13

Beam, Cris. *I Am J*. New York: Little, Brown, 2011.

Friedman, Lauren. "The Stranger-Than-Fiction Story of a Woman Who Was Her Own Twin." *Business Insider*, February 2, 2014, http://www.businessinsider.com/lydia-fairchild-is-her-own-twin-2014-2.

Peters, Julie Anne. *Luna*. New York: Little, Brown, 2006.

Wittlinger, Ellen. *Parrotfish*. New York: Simon & Schuster, 2011.

Yu, Neng et al. "Disputed Maternity Leading to Identification of Tetragametic Chimerism." *New England Journal of Medicine* 346, no. 20 (2002): 1545–52.

## CHAPTER 14

Fletcher, Joseph. *The Ethics of Genetic Control: Ending Reproductive Roulette*. New York: Anchor, 1974.

Glover, Jonathan. *Causing Deaths and Saving Lives*. New York: Penguin, 1991.

Kass, Leon, and James Q. Wilson. *The Ethics of Human Cloning*. Washington, DC: AEI Press, 1998.

## CHAPTER 15

*Document of the Holy See on Human Cloning*, September 27, 2004, http://www.vatican.va/roman_curia/secretariat_state/2004/documents/rc_seg-st_20040927_cloning_en.html.

English, Jane. "What Do Grown Children Owe Their Parents?" In *Having Children*, edited by Onora O'Neill and William Ruddick. New York: Oxford University Press, 1979.

Friedman, Joan A. *The Same but Different: How Twins Can Live, Love, and Learn to Be Individuals*. Santa Monica, CA: Rocky Pines Press, 2014.

Kass, Leon. *Life, Liberty and the Defense of Dignity: The Challenge for Bioethics*. San Francisco: Encounter Books, 2002.

Kohl, Susan. *Twin Stories: The Mysterious and Unique Bond*. Berkeley, CA: Wildcat Canyon Press, 2001.

Segal, Nancy. *Entwined Lives: Twins and What They Tell Us About Human Behavior*. New York: Dutton, 1999.

Wright, Lawrence. *Twins: And What They Tell Us About Who We Are*. New York: John Wiley, 1997.

## CHAPTER 16

Appiah, Kwame Anthony. *The Ethics of Identity*. Princeton, NJ: Princeton University Press, 2005.

Hacking, Ian. "Making Up People." *London Review of Books* 28, no. 16 (August 17, 2006), 23–26.

Sherif, M. et al. *The Robbers Cave Experiment: Intergroup Conflict and Cooperation* (Vol. 10). Norman: University of Oklahoma Press, 1961.

Milgram, Stanley. *Obedience to Authority: An Experimental View*. New York: Harper & Row, 1974.

Zimbardo, Philip. *The Stanford Prison Experiment: A Simulation Study of the Psychology of Imprisonment*. Philip G. Zimbardo, Inc., 1972.

## CHAPTER 17

Rachels, James. "Why Privacy Is Important." *Philosophy and Public Affairs* 4, No. 14 (1975).

Wood, Bari. *Twins.* New York: Signet, 1978.

## CHAPTER 18

Dennett, Daniel. *Elbow Room: The Varieties of Freedom Worth Wanting.* Cambridge, MA: MIT Press, 1984.

Kane, Robert. *Free Will and Values.* Albany: State University of New York Press, 1985.

Watson, Gary, ed. *Free Will.* Oxford, UK: Oxford University Press, 1982.

## CHAPTER 19

Foucault, Michel. *The Birth of the Clinic: An Archaeology of Medical Perception.* New York: Random House, 1973. Originally published as *Naissance de la clinique—une archéologie du regard medical* (Paris: Presses Universitaires de France, 1963).

Foucault, Michel. *The History of Sexuality, Vol. 1: An Introduction.* New York: Pantheon Books, 1978. Originally published as *Histoire de la sexualité, Vol. I: La Volonté de savoir* (Paris: Gallimard, 1976).

Foucault, Michel. *The History of Sexuality, Vol. II: The Use of Pleasure.* New York: Pantheon Books, 1985. Originally published as *Histoire de la sexualité, Vol. II: L'Usage des plaisirs* (Paris: Gallimard, 1984).

Foucault, Michel. *The History of Sexuality, Vol III: The Care of the Self.* New York: Pantheon Books, 1986. Originally published as *Histoire de la sexualité, Vol. III: Le Souci de soi* (Paris: Gallimard, 1984).

Foucault, Michel. *Madness and Civilization: A History of Insanity in the Age of Reason.* London, Tavistock, 1965. Originally published as *Histoire de la folie à l'âge classique—Folie et déraison* (Paris: Plon, 1961).

Foucault, Michel. *The Birth of Biopolitics: Lectures at the Collège de France, 1975–1979.* Hampshire, UK: Palgrave Macmillan.

Foucault, Michel. *Discipline and Punish: The Birth of the Prison*. Translated by Alan Sheridan. New York: Pantheon Books, 1978. Originally published as *Surveiller et punir: Naissance de la prison* (Paris: Gallimard, 1975).

Krakauer, Jon. *Under the Banner of Heaven*. New York: Anchor, 2004.

Szasz, Thomas. *The Myth of Mental Illness: Foundations of a Theory of Personal Conduct*. New York: Harper & Row, 1974.

# Acknowledgments

In writing this book, I gratefully acknowledge the help of my own enthusiastic Clone Club: BS/MD students Joanne Sheraj Jacob and Lakshmi Subramani were early enthusiasts, watched every episode, researched topics, and came up with great ideas; Heather Martin, an amazing reference librarian for the humanities in UAB's Sterne Library, fact-checked many references and had the best recall of details of each episode; Shawn Galin, PhD, an associate professor of medicine, physiology, and biophysics, and director of the endocrinology course in the School of Medicine, made insightful suggestions and corrections, especially about the science; Katrina Barlow, BA, MPA, watched every episode, and despite having to read every word two or three times, proved to be a very astute proofer and observer, as did my BS/MD student, Lillian Chien. Thanks, too, to Trygve Tollefsbol, UAB professor of biology, for answering pesky questions about cloning and telomeres. Leah Wilson, the editor at BenBella, was every writer's dream editor, providing fast, insightful, and good suggestions, as was her able editorial associate, Vy Tran; both also had a passion for the show. I also thank copyeditor James Fraleigh, the most careful and knowledgeable copyeditor I've had in writing dozens of books. Finally, I thank my wife, Patricia Rippetoe, PhD, MA, a BenBella author, for suggesting this project to me and pushing me to do it.

# About the Author

Gregory Pence is an international expert on the ethics of human cloning. A year after the birth of the lamb Dolly in 1997, he wrote *Who's Afraid of Human Cloning?* and in 2004, *Cloning After Dolly: Who's Still Afraid?* In 2000, he was the lone bioethicist to testify before Congress and the California Senate against bills that would have criminalized human cloning. He has talked about cloning humans at endowed lectures in Brazil, Switzerland, and Australia and on many North American campuses.

He has taught for forty years at the University of Alabama at Birmingham (UAB), where he chairs philosophy. For thirty-four years, he taught a required course in bioethics at UAB to 160 medical students, a course that discussed human cloning. His teams have won three national championships in college Ethics Bowls and he has won the two top teaching awards at UAB. His *Medical Ethics* has run seven editions over twenty-five years with McGraw-Hill. He has published over sixty op-ed essays in the *New York Times, Birmingham News, Wall Street Journal, Los Angeles Times,* and *Newsweek,* including many on cloning humans and bioethics.